Storytelling in the Classroom

Enhancing Oral and Traditional Skills
for Teachers

Alison Davies

P·CP

Paul Chapman
Publishing

First published 2007

Paul Chapman Publishing
A SAGE Publications Company
1 Oliver's Yard
55 City Road
London EC1Y 1SP

SAGE Publications Inc.
2455 Teller Road
Thousand Oaks, California 91320

SAGE Publications India Pvt Ltd
B1/I1 Mohan Cooperative Industrial Area
Mathura Road
Post Bag 7,
New Delhi 110 044

SAGE Publications Asia-Pacific Pte Ltd
33 Pekin Street # 2-01
Far East Square
Singapore 048763

www.luckyduck.co.uk

Commissioning editors: Barbara Maines and George Robinson
Illustrator: Philippa Drakeford

British Library Cataloguing in Publication data

A catalogue record for this book is available from the British Library

ISBN 978 1 4129 2025 4

Library of Congress Control Number: 2006904349

Typeset by Pantek Arts Ltd, Maidstone, Kent
Printed on paper from sustainable forests
Printed in Great Britain by Cromwell Press, Trowbridge, Wiltshire

Contents

Part One   Techniques for Teachers

1 Once Upon a Time

Once upon a time there was storytelling. It's hard to pin-point exactly when it started, although I would guess that when man first began to communicate he used stories. Cave paintings of that age are not isolated doodles or pictures etched in stone for amusement; they are tales describing actual events, things that happened at that time. As vocabulary developed so did stories, and perhaps that's why we created such a rich language, so that it could be used instinctively to create tales, to make sense of the world and who we are. Stories are an inherent part of communication. They are essential for survival on many levels. Stop for a moment. Listen. You will hear snippets of conversation, dialogue passing from one person to another. The most common thing you will hear is the recounting of tales. It's what we do on a daily basis. In some cases it's a means of passing on necessary information; but we also use stories as a way of sharing, of explaining who we are to others and forming bonds within society. We use stories to educate, to offer wisdom and knowledge to those less experienced. We are storytellers every day whether we realise it or not and it is a skill that can be developed and used in education with exceptional results.

Records of storytelling have been found in many ancient cultures and languages, including Sanskrit, Old German, Latin, Chinese, Greek, Icelandic and Old Slavonic. The Celtic bards of old used storytelling as a way of making sense of their origins, a way to build a common history. They would chronicle events through poetic narrations, epic tales that are preserved to this day in folklore and legend. Coming from Nottingham, I would cite Robin Hood as the perfect example of this. Medieval literature has many examples of bardic tales and poetry recounting the adventures of Robin and his Merry Men. Is it true? Who knows, but it highlights the potency of such storytelling. In her wonderful analysis of the history of storytelling Anne Pellowski suggests that the oral tradition has its origins in play, with gifted but ordinary folk entertaining their social group. She researched this further and came to the following conclusions, which illustrate the importance of storytelling and how it has evolved throughout history:

1. Storytelling grew from the playful elements of human nature and satisfied a need for self-entertainment. We are gifted with an imagination; we can create something out of nothing. Children do this automatically through imaginary friends and worlds.

2. It fulfilled a need to explain surroundings; the physical world. As humans we are logical creatures, we need to make sense of things, to find the rhyme and reason behind evolution.

3. It evolved through the intrinsic urge to communicate and share experiences. Part of being human is the desire to form bonds, family units etc.

4. It developed as a means of explaining and substantiating the supernatural forces believed to be present in the world at that time, thus satisfying religious beliefs. Again this is partly linked to our need to make some sort of sense of things, even if they appear beyond our understanding.

5. It fulfilled an aesthetic need for beauty, regularity and form through expressive language and music.

6. It was born from a need to record history, to chronicle the deeds of ancestors and in so doing keep them alive for years to come.

It is understandable that this medium of communication is so successful and important, but what exactly are we talking about here? What is storytelling? There are many different definitions and opinions; this is because as an art form it is hard to define. How can you classify something that is flexible, the parameters are always shifting? Anne Pellowski attempts to explain it in her book:

'the art or craft of narration of stories in verse/and or prose, as performed or led by one person before a live audience; the stories narrated may be spoken, chanted, or sung, with or without musical, pictorial, and/or other accompaniment and may be learned from oral, printed or mechanically recorded sources; one of its purposes may be that of entertainment'. (Pellowski, 1991, p. 15)

I like to think of storytelling as a way of lifting words from a page and breathing life into them. I collect stories in my head; most of the time they are original. I like to create new tales and sometimes I write them down, sometimes I don't. As a storyteller I have developed ways of recording my tales visually, in my mind's eye. It's nice to get away from the constraints of the written word – not that there isn't a place for that, there is. I enjoy writing and I think it has immense value, in fact in some cases storytelling has actually helped with my written work. But storytelling allows me to escape the confines of the page. I can add colour and texture to my words and make them flexible. It doesn't matter where I take the tale, because I am the only one that knows it; I am the captain, and the ship is my story. I am taking the audience on a journey. I move through the story, changing pace and style. In essence I am free to do what I want, when I want. I can take the plot in a different direction; I can develop the characters and give them room to grow. If I choose I can use my stories to deliver a particular message, to pass on wisdom and entertain. I can tell the same story ten times and every single time it will be different depending on what I want to focus on. Storytelling is the best tonic for the imagination, and as such children find it exciting and fun. They have permission to go wherever they want, to explore language and learn about life in a safe environment. They immediately connect with the storyteller; there is no book or paper to act as a barrier. The only pictures they have are in their heads. The words become their own.

The difference between storytelling and reading might be a clear one, but why is it so important in the classroom? Here are some reasons why storytelling is essential for educational development and can be used to complement the curriculum:

- Storytelling aids in the development of children's ability to interpret and understand events beyond their immediate experience. Children's perception changes as they 'make it real' and identify with the story on a personal level. They are able to do this in a positive and safe environment. Moral tales are particularly good learning tools as they immerse children in situations where they can learn a lesson; they then discover the truth in their own way.

- Storytelling is a medium of shared experiences. This helps children to empathise with the characters, to feel elated at another's joy, sad for their misfortunes. It is a tool for social and interpersonal development.

- Storytelling aids language development. Children need to be exposed to language to fully understand its implications. This will also have a beneficial effect on reading skills and being able to associate meanings and emotions with words.

- Storytelling helps with listening and speaking skills. Children will learn the importance of listening, of how to communicate ideas and interact with others. They will develop their vocabulary and learn when and where to use words and phrases.

- Storytelling stretches the imagination. It encourages children to escape into a fantasy world, and supports their daydreams, which has positive benefits on mental health and clarity leaving them better able to cope with day-to-day situations (fairy tales are ideally suited for this purpose).

- Storytelling entertains and excites, which is an important part of learning. If children are having fun they are involved, and motivated to learn more. There is nothing more rewarding than watching a class light up with enthusiasm as they engage with your story, and everything falls into place. You can almost see them working through the logical process, anticipating what comes next and discovering the real meaning of the tale.

- Storytelling can be used across the curriculum to break down subjects that are difficult to learn. It can be used to make problem areas more accessible, by adopting a creative attitude and coming at the subject from a different angle. Think how much more appealing it is to say 'Today I'm going to tell you a story about a girl and her mathematical friend,' rather than 'Today we're going to look at data handling and how we can use it as a tool in mathematics.' The first sentence sounds intriguing; immediately questions begin to form in the mind – What girl? Who is her mathematical friend? What happens to them? The second sentence might be informative but it doesn't encourage questions. It is a statement of fact and therefore harder for the children to relate to.

- Storytelling helps children appreciate different cultures, in addition to helping them examine and value their own personal heritage. For example, I use a Navajo Indian story about Quillwork Girl and her seven brothers who flee the Great Buffalo spirit and end up as stars in the night sky. It's a beautiful story that not only illustrates how the Native Americans lived, their traditions and habits, but also their spirituality. They use their stories as a way of communicating their beliefs.

- Storytelling is the natural way to introduce children to the wonderful world of books and reading. It's a good idea to have plenty of reading material available so that the class can do follow up work, and read stories similar to the ones you have been telling. The next stage is for the class to create their own stories and learn how to communicate their ideas individually and in groups.

There's a story I tell in schools called 'The King's Cloak'. This story was handed down to me by another storyteller and a close friend. It's one of the first stories I used in the classroom and it works with any age group every time. This is because not only is it an excellent tale that allows the class to get involved in the telling, it is the perfect introduction to explaining what storytelling is.

When I first heard the bare bones of this tale the ending was different. I took the liberty of changing it for the purpose of storytelling in the classroom, and, as I will explain in future chapters, it is part of the role of the storyteller to develop and change tales that are not necessarily originated personally and find a unique voice.

The King's Tailor is the central character. The story follows events as the Tailor continues to make items of clothing for the King from the same piece of material (a smelly old kitchen rag). The King is very precious about his clothes and incredibly vain (this is what makes the tale amusing). Each time the Tailor makes something he convinces the King that it is something special, so the King wears it over and over, until he wears it out. The Tailor then has to make something new (I get the class to interject with things they think he might make for the King). As the story goes on the items of clothing get smaller and smaller until eventually the Tailor is left with a couple of ragged threads. The question then is what can the tailor create now? The answer is the crux of the story. He takes the threads and weaves them into his hair, and from that day forwards he leaves the palace and spends his life wandering from kingdom to kingdom. He makes a living not by weaving clothes, but by weaving tales, wonderful, colourful yarns that people remember, and his favourite tale is that of the King's Cloak. This illustrates the concept of handing down tales, of using them to pass on information and to record history. I could explain this to the class, but I prefer to show rather than tell; the children then come to an understanding by connecting with the tale, and that, in essence, is what storytelling is all about.

How to use this book

In the following chapters you will find information on storytelling, getting started as a storyteller and how to implement this ancient oral tradition in the classroom. This book is a practical guide with tips for teachers on developing storytelling skills with the intention of running activities in class. It is aimed at teachers of pupils of all ages (although the nature of storytelling seems to appeal best to those at primary level). There are lesson plans and ideas that can be incorporated at any phase of the curriculum. The activities vary and it is quite possible to mix and match these ideas to suit the age and needs of your particular class. Storytelling is a flexible tool, and should be used as such, so take the bits you think will work for you and modify them. Happy storytelling!

2 The Path of the Storyteller

You can see the benefits of using storytelling in the classroom; you know what it's about and how it can be used. Now comes the exciting bit – finding and creating a tale to tell! It sounds a challenge, but there are ways and means to make the process easy and enjoyable. The most important part is choosing the right tale for your audience. As a teacher you have the added advantage of knowing your audience, of being aware of their strengths and weaknesses and being able to work with these. Your next decision is whether to choose a tale from the wealth of material available for your audience, or whether to create something specifically for the task in hand. Both options have their advantages.

Choosing a tale

As a fledgling storyteller you might prefer the option of finding a tale. The benefit here is that you know the story works, it's already formed and it's in print. What better feasibility test than a tale that's already out there and being enjoyed? Some storytellers prefer to adapt other people's stories; this takes away the pressure of creating something that might not be a success. The story doesn't lose anything by not being original because every storyteller has his or her own style. The same story can be told by ten storytellers and each time it will be different.

Here are some tips to help you locate the perfect story for telling.

1 Pick a tale that you enjoy

You might have something in mind. Most storytellers agree the right tale seems to find its owner, in other words, you will recognise the one for you. It may jump out at you, but don't worry if not. It can take time to find what you are looking for. The tale you pick must resonate. It must connect with you the storyteller, because then, and only then, will you be able to do it justice

9

and deliver it with a level of integrity. It is absolutely no use picking a tale because you think it imparts the right message or for educational value only. If it doesn't fill you with a burning desire to tell, then it will come across as limp and one-dimensional and any educational value will be lost. The best advice for any storyteller is to enjoy the tale. If you have fun with it, so will your audience. No amount of fancy presentation skill can cover up the fact that you don't actually like the tale, and if you don't like it, you can't expect anyone else to.

I love the tale 'The King's Cloak' that I mentioned in Chapter 1. However, when I first told that tale I stuck rigidly to the version I had heard, and although the beginning and middle moved smoothly, I wasn't happy with the ending. There was no conclusion, or meaning underlined, and because of this it didn't sit easy with me when I told it. I didn't enjoy the last bit, which naturally came across to my audience, who also looked a little puzzled and disappointed with the conclusion. I've since re-worked the tale and told it many times and I thoroughly enjoy myself. I particularly like the new ending I have given it because it makes sense. It resonates with me and that comes across.

2 Know your audience

Finding a story to suit your audience is a little like finding a pair of shoes; it has to be the right fit. The only way to ensure this is to know your audience, to know their interests, attention span, likes, dislikes, previous experience with stories, level of literacy etc. You will have an idea of the type of activities your class enjoys, work on this. Look at the kind of reading material available; take note of the stories that are read repeatedly and the ones that get ignored. Think about possible themes that appeal to your class. What worked well in the past? Do they like magic/fantasy or horror, or do they prefer funny tales? Think about what you want to get across; is there a specific lesson that you would like them to learn? If so, which of the above genres is best suited to the message? For example, you may decide you want to touch upon bullying and peer pressure. In that case it clearly wouldn't be wise to use a farcical story that is littered with hilarious events; this would detract from the heartbeat of the tale. A little laughter could be incorporated, but not to the point that it overshadows the real meaning. Having said that, there are times when serious issues can be highlighted by putting the characters and the plot into a different genre. A story about bullying might work well in a magical land where the class can identify with the characters and connect with the tale because it stirs the imagination.

3 Breathe new life into old tales

Don't be afraid to use the tried and tested. Fairy tales (or wonder tales as they were originally called) have lasted because they are potent and deal with relevant issues. The Brothers Grimm got the recipe just right with their darkly magical tales, which did ironically reflect their name (if you examine the bare bones of their stories). These tales embraced light and darkness, they touched on universal fears, hopes and aspirations. There are hundreds of books on fairy tales and a wide range of material to choose from, so this is a good option for your first storytelling session. Fairy tales have morals. There is much to be learnt about stories, and life, from something as simple as 'Cinderella'. Many fairy tales have their roots in folk tales and legends and it's interesting to go back and discover elements of the familiar in the Celtic classics. You will find that the earlier 'wonder tales' were more gruesome than their modern counterparts, but the essence of the tale and its lesson are still evident today.

Don't be afraid to take an old tale and change it to suit your needs, or your audience. You have poetic licence to play with the words and the plot. You adopt your own way of telling, which brings a different flavour to the tale. The Miller's Daughter might become the daughter of a local baker, the travelling healer, a district nurse. To make the story fun you could ask the children to think of modern alternatives to fairy tale characters. What might they do now, and what would they be called? Having said that, children enjoy the tradition and romance of fairy tales; they enjoy hearing about kings and queens, dragons and witches. They want to know about the ancient curse and the glass slipper, or the princess who couldn't sleep on a pea. They want to know about the Witch and the Seven Dwarves and what happened when the Wolf met Little Red Riding Hood. Remember, archetypes create wonderful pictures and will help you to instantly connect with your audience. It may seem old hat to you, but it's new and exciting to a child.

4 Choose the best

Children deserve the best. Pick stories that make sense and have a satisfying ending. There's nothing worse than a group of blank faces at the end of a tale. You want them to understand the story, and feel satisfied with its conclusion. Make sure that any questions are answered, any points are made clear. Pick stories where something happens. Look out for interesting characters that the children can identify with and plots that are exciting. Remember, children relate to children; they do not want to hear about adults going on great quests, no matter how exhilarating this seems. They have to be able to put themselves in the story. Test your selections on the type of audience for which you intend to use it. Refine it to suit their needs. You will find as you progress that certain elements appeal and work well. Make a mental note of these and use the same device in other tales. For example, repetition always works well with children; it gives them something to latch on to, something to draw them into the story and involve them. See for example, 'The King's Cloak' and 'The Water Lord' in Part Two. If your story of choice does not have any sentences of repetition (i.e. spells or chants that the children can join in with) don't be afraid to add this element in. Play around with words and see what happens.

5 Find a tale that suits your style

Every storyteller has a different voice. You may discover that you prefer to tell your tales in the first person. Perhaps you feel more comfortable with modern tales rather than fairy tales. You may find humour difficult, but have a natural aptitude for spooky atmospheric tales. Read your story aloud. How does it sound to you? Do you struggle with long passages? Does it flow off the tongue and feel right? You might discover the perfect Navajo Indian tale but find that the phrases are short and inexpressive, or perhaps you prefer the no-nonsense uncluttered approach. Listen to audio tapes of stories, go and see storytellers perform, it will give you a clearer idea of what works.

I have a very descriptive style; I like stories where I can create atmosphere and tension through my voice. I also like stories that allow me to use my voice in different ways, which often means lots of interesting characters. A fable would be too sparse for me; I would have to create a story around this and use interesting words to build up the picture. Other storytellers I know, however, prefer to use plain language at a faster pace.

Creating a tale

This is not as difficult as it sounds, and can be very rewarding. There are many benefits in creating your own tale to tell. For a start, that tale is original, it may have elements of other stories, but it is your tale, and as such has never been heard or read before. You are the master of the tale and that provides an extra boost of confidence and control. You will feel happier chopping and changing bits, and you will find that you can be flexible with the plot and characters. This is much easier to do with your own creation. When you write your own tale you can tailor it to suit your requirements. Rather than spending time searching for the perfect tale to do what you want, make it do what you want, write it to fulfil your needs. You will also find that learning your tale is an easier task. When you use someone else's work it is easy to get caught up in their words. Instead of making the tale your own, logic dictates that the way it is written is the right way to tell it. This is not necessarily the case, but if you have ownership of the story then you are giving yourself permission to relax and express yourself freely.

So where do you start? Do you wait for inspiration to strike? Here are some easy ways to stimulate your imagination and get the words flowing.

1 Memories

Think of important events in your life, significant things that happened in your childhood. Think about positive experiences. Rather than trying to list them in your head or on paper, draw them. Take a sheet of paper and draw a picture, a still that sums up what that memory means to you. For example, I remember a day when I was a child and we were at the seaside. We were in the camp club and my parents were sitting at a table. I was gazing out of the window when I spotted a huge bumble bee sitting on the ledge. I remember thinking how furry and soft that bumble bee looked and even though I knew they stung people, I still reached out my hand to stroke its back. Of course the inevitable happened and it stung me, but I didn't cry. If I were to draw this experience I would draw a picture of a girl with her hand outstretched towards the window sill and a bee.

Now think about how you would describe this picture without telling the story behind it. There are three types of language you would use – description, action and emotion. Try to describe the picture using each type of language separately. So in the case of my picture if I were to use the language of description I might say 'The sky was blue and the sun was out', 'The bee was fat and furry', 'The room was filled with tables and chairs' etc. Keep it simple. Imagine the picture you are describing is a painting in a gallery. If I were to describe my picture using the language of action I might say 'The trees were blowing in the wind', 'The sun blazed a trail through the sky', 'The bee fluttered its wings' etc. Finally, if I were to use the language of emotion I might say 'I felt excited, and a little bit sorry for the bee'. You will notice that it is very difficult to separate the types of language, and that your natural inclination is to move on with the story and use all three. This is an important exercise as it will make you think about the words you use, and how it is important to incorporate description, action and emotion if you want to create a good tale. Description sets the scene, action gets the story moving and emotion adds colour and depth.

Now take your story and turn it into a fairy tale. In effect you are putting it into a more accessible genre for children. Think about the way fairy tales are formed, and the kind of words that are used. In the case of my story a young girl might become a little princess. The bee might be a magical bumble bee, and the room might be the tower room of a castle. Fairy tales always have elements of good and evil, and there is usually a moral. Think about your story, does it have a moral? Was a lesson learned? Can you introduce good and evil? Most importantly what is the heartbeat of the tale? If you could describe it in one word, what would that word be? I might want to make my story a tale about overcoming fear (essentially that's what it was). In that case I might take the little princess and make her shy and lonely. Perhaps she never goes out of her tower room, until the day that the magical bumble bee lands on her ledge. Then after touching the bee it's like a spell lifts and she is filled with happiness and confidence. The bee might disappear and she might decide to go out in search of it, and from there she might meet other children and make friends. Of course the tale would need some kind of resolution, and adventure. I might decide to introduce a wicked witch. Perhaps the bee is a young boy who's been cursed and when the little princess reaches out to stroke him the curse is broken. Once you start piecing your tale together you will find there are so many paths you can take. One story might lead you into another.

Get your class to make a memory box. You could either have a central memory box for the entire class, or one per group. Get them to dress it up with glitter and colour and make it look as special as possible. This will be the place where they are going to store their happiest/funniest memories. Then get each child to write a memory or draw a picture to represent something that happened to them that they enjoyed (a picture and a couple of key words are sufficient for this exercise). It may be a special holiday they had, or a birthday, or a day when they did something that they felt good about. Now in pairs get them to share their memories. This will give them confidence to tell their tale and get them used to speaking and listening. Each child then places a memory in the memory box and recounts the tale of what happened to them. When there are enough memories stored in the box ask the children either in groups or individually to pick out a different memory and describe what they see, or what is written on the paper. Encourage them to get creative with each other's tales and come up with new tales for the pictures. You may find lots of ideas for stories. It is interesting to see how the children relate to their memories and how they choose to re-tell these events.

2 Pictures

Pictures are a great source of inspiration. Storytellers work in pictures, so putting a story together based on pictures or paintings or photographs is a good way of thinking visually.

Keep an eye out for interesting pictures, with characters and settings that can be elaborated. Take a trip to a local gallery. Look through old photographs. Browse illustrated children's books and look at the pictures rather than attempting to read the story. You may see something completely different in the drawing, and come up with your own interpretation of events. Pictures are snapshots of events; they capture what is going on for one second of that story. Take that snapshot and build your own story.

Ask yourself the following questions:

- Where is the picture set? Is this another country, a world or land?

- Who are the people in the picture? What are they doing? Why are they in this situation? How are they feeling? What has brought them to this place? What are their names? Where do they live? What is their motivation? Are they happy or sad, angry or excited?

- What will happen next? If you draw another picture, what might be happening in that? How will things change? What is the outcome?

Give the picture a title, now imagine you are going to tell the tale using all of the information you have uncovered. This technique works for any kind of art form. I once worked with a sculpture in a school. I wanted to create a story that explored the many facets of the piece and encouraged the children to get something from it. I noted down everything I could see. I thought about what that sculpture represented and what the children might see when they looked at it. I then placed it in another world and my tale began. I suggested different characters that might live in the sculpture and what might happen to them and from there the children were able to build stories which grew in so many diverse directions. It was a motivational tool not only for my own story creation but for the class too. The story I created is called 'Spot the Difference' in Part Two. It shows how something produced in one art form can develop into another, and become an entertaining and informative tale.

3 Other stories

It is perfectly acceptable to incorporate other stories into the tale you tell. You may be looking for a tried and tested formula: for example, the standard format of good versus evil that is used so well in fairy tales can be adapted. You can borrow characters and tell the story from their perspective. What happened to Sleeping Beauty whilst she was asleep? Where did she go? What did she dream? What were her adventures? Perhaps she learnt something during that time. You may begin to tell her tale and then ask your class to come up with their version of events.

4 Games of chance

This is one you can do with your class. Get them to create stories by using a simple game of chance. You can use a number of techniques to determine the path of your tale, the characters and the general theme.

You will need a sheet of possible options for the story, and a square for each which allows for a yes or no, heads or tails result (see below). Then by using the simple flick of a coin between heads and tails you can determine which way the story will go. A coin works well when you want to keep the story geared to a particular subject. If you need to provide more choices then you could use a dice, or even a spinner with a selection of options written on paper.

The simple exercise below offers three possible options for a story. It's a fun exercise to do in groups, to get them started in creating storyboards.

Character 1	H/T	Character 2	H/T	Setting	H/T
Boy	Heads	Wizard	Heads	Woods	Heads
Girl	Tails	Prince	Tails	Jungle	Tails

If you wanted to make the exercise really fun you could challenge your class to an unrehearsed storytelling session. They flick the coins and make the choices for the story and you then create and tell the tale, there and then, from the information you have. This sounds difficult but it's actually easy once you start, and I guarantee there will be pupils queuing up to have a go. You could even start the story, set the scene from the results you have been given and then ask members of your class to take it in turns to continue.

5 Other perspectives

Take a story you know well and see it from another angle. Take an inanimate object and imagine what it sees and feels. What role does it have to play in the story? Give it a personality. Remember that it will be present for only part of the original tale, so it will have a totally different perspective of events. It will have its own story.

Take a smaller character from a popular tale and tell his or her story. Who is Cinderella's Fairy Godmother? Where did she come from? How did she feel? How did the sequence of events look to her? Again these are all questions you can put to your class to get them thinking creatively. I particularly like to get children thinking about inanimate objects and breathing life into them. What's it like to be a tree? Imagine what a tree might see? Perhaps it lives in a magic forest, perhaps it is the tree in the forest where the Wolf chases Red Riding Hood? There are so many options with this exercise. You can develop a network of related stories from one traditional tale.

Try this in class

Choose a fairy tale, Red Riding Hood for example. Get the class to draw a picture that represents this tale. The picture would include the main characters; this will form the centre of your display. Now split the class into groups and get them to take a different character or inanimate object from the story – they might choose to tell the tale from the perspective of the Wolf, or a tree in the wood, the cloak Red Riding Hood wears, even the bed her Grandmother sleeps in. All of these things will have different tales to tell. Get the children to draw pictures to tell their version of events. They can write a short narrative, a couple of sentences, underneath each picture to describe what is happening. When they have finished you will find you have an array of pictures and tales, which when positioned around the original story make for a colourful story map and display. This is a simple way to show how a plot develops and how sub-plots exist and grow from strands of the story.

Stories are in everything, and once you begin the creative process you will find the strangest things stir you into action. I once wrote a story that was inspired by something that had been said in a gardening programme on TV. The presenter was talking about a garden perennial called 'Devil's Guts' and how its leafy roots cling to everything in sight. The name of the plant, and its constitution, struck a chord in me, and from there the first line of my story was born. It continued to grow (a little like the plant in question). The story, 'October Eyes', is in my first book, *Small Deaths*, and is a firm favourite when I do spooky storytelling evenings for adults.

3 Don't Lose the Plot!

Now that you have your story, whether it is an original piece or something tried and tested, the next step is learning how to remember it for performance. After all, this is storytelling, you will not be reading your story from a book. This defeats the object. The book or paper becomes a barrier, a block between you and your audience. The whole point of storytelling in the classroom is to engage with the children and motivate them and you can only do this by interacting on a personal level.

Remembering a tale from scratch may sound difficult but there are techniques that every storyteller uses to recall a piece. The most important thing to say here is do not try to learn your story word for word. You are *telling* your tale, not reciting it. If you learn the story like an actor learns lines it may seem impressive, but if you then forget a line or a word this can throw you and your entire tale could collapse. This is also not a good example for the class. You want them to enjoy the freedom of expressing themselves without the worry of remembering things in a word-perfect, parrot-like fashion. Storytelling is an interactive experience, it's something that your class can enjoy together and be a part of. If you learn your tale verbatim then any interaction from the class becomes disruptive as you will have no choice but to stick to a rigid format.

Work in pictures

Storytellers constantly work with pictures. We see the story as we tell it. I compare this to watching a video in my head and then relaying the details. Visualising my tale not only helps to keep me on the right track, but I also feel as if I am there, and the story becomes real for me. This is key when working with children. You can't expect them to believe anything unless you truly believe it. If you are there in the story, then they will be too, and the connection is made. So whether it is ghosts and goblins or giants and dragons, if I'm telling a tale in the classroom I live every second of it in my head. I fight the evil witch, I scale the castle wall, I trick the king into giving up his fortune, even if it's all in my mind.

It's amazing the amount of information you can recall if you picture it rather than trying to remember it. Everyone learns in a different way. Some people prefer to think in lists, others can learn things parrot fashion, but it's surprising how much you can take in if you visualise it.

Try this in class

Get your class to sit in a large circle. You are going to play a memory game which is very much an exercise in accelerated learning. Tell your class to picture the scene as if they are looking at a painting in a gallery. Begin by saying 'In my playground there is a gate, and just in front of that gate is a …' then add in an item. It can be anything, from something that you would expect to find in a playground like a football net, or a climbing frame, to something silly like a pink elephant, or a giant ice-cream! Encourage them to use their imaginations; the more absurd the items are, the easier they are to picture. Get them to think about colour, and expression, this will give the image vitality. Once an object or thing has been placed in the picture it cannot be moved. This is a painting and everything that appears must stay in the same position, it is static. Now go around the circle asking each child to place something new in the picture. Before they do this, they must run through the other items that have been placed, so they must start from the beginning and try to recall each thing. Suggest that they close their eyes, and see the picture; this helps them to retain the information. Go around the circle at least twice. You will be amazed at the amount of information your class can remember.

Use a story ladder

I suggest a ladder because this is how I remember stories. I visualise this ladder in my head, and sometimes if the story is particularly complicated I write it down in the form of a story ladder (see the illustration on page 22).

A story ladder is like any ladder, it helps you climb from A to B. It helps you navigate the landscape of your tale, making sense of the locations and the different routes you might take to get there. At first when you use the ladder it may appear a direct route to the final sentence of your tale, but you can take as many steps as you like to reach your destination. As you get more accustomed you will find it is quite natural to add steps and deviate from the most direct path. Using story ladders or maps might seem unnecessary, but it's a very good exercise that not only helps you to remember your tale and become more confident with it, but also to dissect the plot and discover what is at the heart of the story. This is very important if you want to deliver a message.

The first time I used this way of mapping a story was with a tale called 'First Date', a dark (almost horror) tale I perform to adults. I wrote the story years ago, and then decided to learn it for performance, but after doing the story ladder exercise with the help of another storyteller I learnt something new about the power of the tale, and the message I wanted to deliver. Now whenever I perform that story I am more aware of what I want to say, and what I want my audience to get from the piece. That in turn makes me give a confident, polished performance.

In a way, story ladders are like maps or plans that help you get under the skin of your tale. Think of it in terms of a real ladder. When you reach the top rung you can see everything, you have taken each step in order and are now at the summit and ready to take in the overall view. In effect, you know the story, you have travelled the path, so now that you have reached the end, you can see it for what it is. You have a clearer idea of what the story means for you, and what message you want to deliver with this tale. From this vantage point you can make an informed judgement.

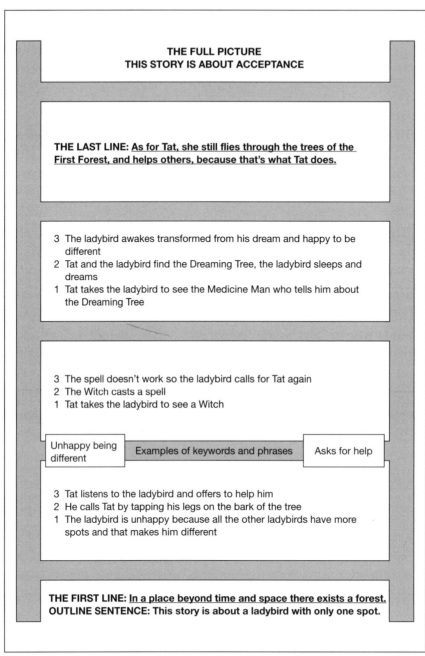

THE FULL PICTURE
THIS STORY IS ABOUT ACCEPTANCE

THE LAST LINE: <u>As for Tat, she still flies through the trees of the First Forest, and helps others, because that's what Tat does.</u>

3 The ladybird awakes transformed from his dream and happy to be different
2 Tat and the ladybird find the Dreaming Tree, the ladybird sleeps and dreams
1 Tat takes the ladybird to see the Medicine Man who tells him about the Dreaming Tree

3 The spell doesn't work so the ladybird calls for Tat again
2 The Witch casts a spell
1 Tat takes the ladybird to see a Witch

Unhappy being different	Examples of keywords and phrases	Asks for help

3 Tat listens to the ladybird and offers to help him
2 He calls Tat by tapping his legs on the bark of the tree
1 The ladybird is unhappy because all the other ladybirds have more spots and that makes him different

THE FIRST LINE: <u>In a place beyond time and space there exists a forest.</u>
OUTLINE SENTENCE: This story is about a ladybird with only one spot.

An example of a story ladder

This is how you create a story ladder. Take a piece of A4 paper, draw a rectangle at the bottom of the page, beneath this rectangle write a sentence that outlines what the story is about in simple terms. In the rectangle you are going to right three or four sentences to outline what happens in the beginning of your story. This is your first step on the ladder, and on this step you set the scene. If it helps, write your first sentence beneath your first step and underline this. This is the ground. This is where your story starts. This sentence should have enough power to make you and your listener want to step onto the ladder of the story.

Draw your next rectangle above this first step. This is the middle section of your story and the next step. Write three or four sentences to outline what happens at this stage in the tale. This step should move your story forward; it should include action and any problems that need to be solved. Don't get bogged down with details, remember this is the bare bones; you don't want to overload your steps.

Leave another space and then draw another rectangle. This is the final step on your ladder. Write three or four sentences in this space to describe what happens in the final stage of your story. Remember, this is the section where any problems are resolved and a conclusion is made. Think of a clear ending to your tale. Write the last sentence above your rectangle and underline it. You do not want to leave your listeners (or yourself) in any doubt as to whether the story has finished, otherwise they (and you) will stretch for the next step and end up floundering in mid air. You want to make it clear that the story has reached a resolute ending that you are happy with.

Draw lines between each of your steps. These lines hold your ladder together and everything in place. Think about any keywords or phrases that will help you to move the story along and write them along these lines – these keywords will help to hold your story together. Finally, when you reach the top of your ladder take a deep breath and look around. How does the story feel, what can you see now you have reached the end? Looking back at each step you might remember things that didn't seem obvious when you first created your piece. At the top of your page write a word or phrase that describes the true heart of your tale.

If your tale is particularly long and complex you may wish to add further steps to your ladder, but only write a couple of lines to represent each stage. This is a guide, the skeleton of your tale, it is up to you to flesh this out, to put meat on the bones.

Learn key phrases

Although you do not want to learn your story verbatim, there is nothing wrong with developing some key phrases. I always suggest that you know the first and last line of your piece. You want a good strong beginning to launch into your tale, so a definite sentence which sets the scene and puts you and your audience in the right frame of mind for the tale is a must. Something like, 'She met him off the train that day. The sluggish scrape of boot leather echoed from the cobalt grey of the platform.'

Immediately, we are there in the story. We don't know who 'she' is, but we know she is at a train station and that she is meeting someone. We can hear the echo of her boots against the platform. In one sentence we have a person, a place and a feeling, and hopefully this is enough to make the audience want to know more. If, however, I had said 'The woman waited on the platform for the train to stop. She was waiting for a man,' we would have the same information, in two sentences, but without the feeling or the impact. We are observing the story, rather than being instantly drawn into the plot. Remember the key to short stories, whether writing or performing them, is to get straight in there with the action. Yes you can set the scene, but don't labour over lengthy descriptions. You have limited words, and in the case of storytelling, limited time. You must capture the attention of your audience and hold it. They do not have the luxury of the book in front of them, so they cannot re-read long paragraphs of description.

I might want to say, 'Clouds gathered in their thousands, row upon row of weary, bloated fists, with their ominous threat to explode in a myriad of different directions and drench the earth with tears.' But this is very wordy, and although I like my descriptions I'm conscious of the fact that this is too convoluted. It might be better to say, 'Clusters of clouds hung like fists, threatening to drown the earth with their tears'. We still have the same atmosphere, the same powerful image of meaty clouds about to explode and tears falling upon the earth, but we've used 14 words instead of 30.

If your language is too complex then you will not connect with your audience, especially if they are children. Think about the type of language they use, and what might intrigue them. They cannot take time over your words. Consider this when thinking about how to start and end your tale.

The way you finish your story should leave the right message with your audience. It is like cooking a fine meal, you want your food (and all three courses) to leave your guests with a good taste in their mouth, you want them to leave the table feeling satisfied, indulged and delighted at the culinary experience they've just had. Storytelling is exactly the same, whatever the age of your audience. In my story 'The Butterfly Boy' I wanted to cover a number of issues: how it feels to be different (in this case the boy has a skin blistering condition) and how physical difficulties might prevent you from doing certain things, but there are no limits with the imagination. This, to me, was the important moral of the tale. So I finished my story with the following two sentences:

'This window is my favourite spot. It opens up into my garden, and into other worlds too; worlds that I can return to any time I want – with a little imagination.'

Through my character's thoughts I illustrated the freedom of the imagination and how wonderful it is to explore. I wanted to create a magical feeling, and to show how this can be done by using the mind.

I always imagine that the last sentence of my story is underlined. Try it. Take a pen in your mind and make it prominent. If you want to make your audience think then leave them with a poignant last sentence, something that opens up the floor for discussion. In the tale 'The King's Cloak' I use the following sentence to draw my tale to a close:

'For the beauty of tales is that they grow just like the threads in the tailor's hair. They become something new and colourful, something timeless.'

I then ask the class what they think. Do they agree that stories are important? What do they think stories might be used for? What kind of stories do they like telling, or listening to? This leads to an interesting discussion on language and storytelling as a historical tradition.

Children in particular expect certain things from a story. They want to feel they understand the meaning, the natural progression of the plot. Make sure that they are satisfied with your conclusion. If it doesn't sound right to you, it won't sound good to them.

Take your first and last line and write them down (as we did with the idea of the story ladder). The act of writing will help to imprint these words upon your mind. Now think about what might come in the middle. Are there phrases you can use to move the story along (a little like the lines that connect the story ladder)? Work towards various points in the story, have three or four set lines if it helps, but then improvise in the direction you take to reach these. This way you have a framework, how you build upon the framework is up to you, and it doesn't matter if it's slightly different each time you tell it.

Have an 'escape sentence'. Create a phrase that can be used at any point in your story should you lose your way. This will be a sentence that doesn't move the story along, or impart information, it just allows you time to breathe and think. Something like 'and so it was, as it is with all things in magical worlds'. This escape sentence doesn't actually add to the plot but it will buy you time to think about where your story is going. As long as you have your key sentences in place, a strong beginning and a good ending, you will be amazed at how easily the story flows.

Practice

It is very important that you practise your tale. Familiarise yourself not only with the words you want to use, but how they sound. Things sound different when they are vocalised. Run through the story and if there are any problem areas work on them. Make sure you have your key phrases and bridges in place in case you lose your way. You wouldn't give a performance in a theatre without practising. You may be in a classroom delivering the story to your class, but you still have an audience, and a very demanding one at that. Your class deserves the best; they will respond more favourably to a polished piece. If you look uncomfortable, then you will pass this unease to your audience, and in turn they will lose interest in your tale. If you look confident, and enjoy every moment of the story, then your class will enjoy it too.

4 It's the Way They Tell Them!

So now you have the story; you have the idea and the characters and you know what you want to achieve in the classroom. But how do you make this story interesting and exciting for children? Storytelling works because you engage with your audience. They connect with your story and see it in their mind's eye, but in order for them to do this they must first connect with you. You are the mouthpiece for the tale. You may stand behind the story, but you are the first point of contact, and therefore how you deliver it is of paramount importance. Think for a moment about the job of a company receptionist. He or she sits at a front desk in the company's reception area. They commandeer the phone and receive all visitors. Your first impression of that company comes from this person. If they are sloppy and disinterested then that's the opinion you will form of the company regardless of how efficient it is. The damage has been done, and although the firm may redeem itself your initial impression will colour your viewpoint from this time onwards.

As a storyteller you are the spokesperson for that story. You need to consider your audience. You may want them to get the most out of your story, but they can only do this if they are interested. Therefore it is up to you to represent that story in the best way possible (this applies whether you are dealing with adults or children). I have seen fantastic stories fall flat because the storyteller fails to do them justice in their presentation. On the flip side, I have also seen mediocre stories shine because they are delivered in an exciting and vibrant manner.

Engaging with your audience is not as difficult as it sounds, especially as there are some useful tools that are very readily available – indeed you could say they are almost at your fingertips.

Voice

Voice is the primary tool. Treat it with respect. Think of it like a synthesiser which you can adapt to any situation. Imagine if all music were the same; if there were no contrast in tone or rhythm; if everything happened in the same key. How boring would that be? Consider this when delivering your story.

Try this yourself

- Note points in the tale where you can introduce light and dark. Are there any scary moments where you can drop the tone of your voice? Any happy moments where you can lighten this? There might be elements of drama where you can turn up the volume and speed.

- Think about the characters. What would they sound like? How will you show the difference in personality? If there is an old witch in your tale remember to illustrate this with your voice, speaking with a raspy, screeching tone, for instance. If there is a giant, you might want to use a slow, booming voice to illustrate his size. You might want to ask your class to join in. Get them to repeat phrases in character, get them thinking about how that character would speak. This is a fun way for them to be involved in the telling of the tale, and it will also help when they come to think of characters for their own stories. They should understand the difference between knowing when to speak and when to listen.

- Consider the pace of the story. As you run through it take note of passages where there's lots of action. When delivering the tale you may want to speed these areas up, to depict frantic activity (coupled with movement this is an effective way to create an exciting atmosphere). Are there parts of your tale that are poignant or sad? Perhaps there's a specific message delivered, a moral or lesson that you want the class to learn. In these areas you could slow down your pace and speak clearly so that the message is heard. Don't be afraid of silence. A moment's pause is very effective, particularly if you want to say something important. It also gives you time to gather your thoughts, so that you say the right thing, with enough emphasis.

Remember: a pause underlines your sentence

Try this in class

Repetition of key phrases always works well in storytelling with children. Not only are they involved in the tale, they become a part of it. They will listen and anticipate what comes next and when they should intervene. Try to find a phrase or sentence that you can use over again in your story. There may be one that already sticks out, or it may be that you have to create such a phrase; something as simple as a piece of conversation that is said by the same character. I use this cheeky phrase in my story about the King and his cloak: 'Oh sir, oh your majesty, don't you look a dandy!' It's simple and silly and the children remember it. I also adopt a wacky high-pitched voice when I say it, which the children try to emulate. You may want to pick one of your characters, and have the children repeat something in the style of that character. A witch's cackle, a pirate's 'Ahoy there!'. Think of anything small and simple and couple it with an interesting use of voice and it will be effective.

Another tip that works well as a spin-off exercise is to get the class to create rhymes, ditties or poems that can be used by the characters in your story. For example, if I was telling 'Cinderella', I would split the class into groups and encourage them to create a spell in the form of a short rhyme that the Fairy Godmother could say when she conjures up Cinderella's ball gown. Or perhaps there would be a phrase that the Prince repeats each time he asks a maiden to try on the glass slipper, or a chant that the Ugly Sisters sing to Cinderella, something wicked to put her in her place. It might be that some groups would like to write a poem about Cinderella, who she is, where she comes from and how she feels. Others might choose to sum up the story in rhyme, or perhaps to take another character like the Fairy Godmother or an Ugly Sister and create a poem for them. There are so many options with this exercise that it's nice to let the groups choose whichever direction they want to take. I would then ask the groups to perform their poem or song to the rest of the class.

Expression

Facial expression goes hand in hand with voice technique. We do this in normal conversation every day. If we are describing something unpleasant our face will support our commentary by providing a grim expression.

By the same token, if we are describing a joyful event our faces demonstrate this with a happy smile. If you can visualise the tale, and feel yourself moving through the emotions, you will have little problem with this. It's a natural part of communication. The difference between storytelling to children and adults is that adults pick up on the nuances; they catch the slight expressions that infer things. Children do not. Consider children's humour. For a child to 'get' a joke it has to be overtly obvious and silly, verging on slapstick. They will not pick up on subtleties within a tale so there will be times that you have to exaggerate your expressions in order to make things clear. This may feel strange. Adults are more inhibited than children and so to do this often means stepping outside of the comfort zone but it is worth it. To captivate a child you have to think like a child, you have to develop a child-like sense of fun, and although this may be difficult in the first instance, it is incredibly liberating.

Try this yourself

Think of your face as just another tool that you use to tell your tale. Imagine that your face is elastic (although I'm not suggesting you 'do a Jim Carey', although he is an excellent example of a performer who relates to children). Stand in front of a mirror and tell your story. Watch your expressions change. Is there an obvious shift from one facial expression to another? Try going over points in the story and making these expressions more extreme. Think of it like donning a mask and have fun! Practise silly expressions. If you enjoy yourself within the tale, then so will your audience. Storytelling for children gives you licence to be silly, to shed some of the constraints of adulthood and remember what it was like to be a child. I do a story about a Sea Witch who is a particularly unsavoury character. I love to twist my face into all sorts of weird contortions to reflect her ugliness. I stoop, with one arm hanging and one at my waist and I screw my face up and lick my lips. Immediately the class know that I'm something pretty hideous and they relate to it.

Remember to keep eye contact. Your audience is not at your feet or in the air. Direct your words and expressions at them, rather than letting them float above their heads. Get down to their level.

Movement and posture

When delivering any kind of presentation it's important to have a good posture and stance. If you are in front of an audience, of whatever age, you need to command their attention. If you slouch, shoulders hunched, head down, with your hands fumbling you look vulnerable and nervous and this will make your audience feel uncomfortable. If, however, you take to the stage/floor with your head up, shoulders back, feet a comfortable distance apart, making constant, unwavering eye contact you give the impression of someone who is confident and competent. Your audience are immediately alert and attentive as they can see that you have something important to say (the same goes for sitting, although I far prefer the flexibility of standing as it allows for more expressive movement). Remember, the class are there to listen and learn, so take control of the situation, take them by the hand and lead them through the story.

Again the most important thing is to use the tools you have to engage with the class. Watch a child telling a tale to their friends, something as small as recounting what happened in the playground at lunch time. I guarantee they will not stand timidly with their hands clasped and their head down mumbling the words. They will be leaping about, using their arms, their legs, every part of their body to demonstrate what happened.

They are active, imaginative storytellers, and so to connect with your class you have to adopt a similar technique. Do not be afraid of your body. Stand tall, stretch out with your arms and legs, jump around if the tale requires it. You are the focal point, what you do must be entertaining enough to keep the attention.

Try this yourself

Think about the characters in your story. How would they stand and walk? What would they be wearing? If, for example, you had a king, you might want to strut with your head held high (your crown balancing on your brow) and your cloak swishing about your ankles. Perhaps there is a small boy who finds himself lost in the woods in your tale (as in the Tat Rootwhistle tale 'Second Chances' included in Part Two). Think about how you would illustrate this in movement. You might want to show this by shrinking your posture, shaking with fear, looking from left to right and over your shoulder. Describe him and back this up with movement so that the children can develop a picture. Put your energies into keeping the story alive; make every movement larger than life.

Try this in class

This is an excellent way to get the class involved in storytelling. Find a part in the story that involves movement. This should not be difficult, since most stories have some sort of action sequence or prominent character that can be defined by a movement. For example, in the story about The King's Cloak every time the King walks the streets of his kingdom and the people see him they bow and curtsy. I always ask the class to help me at this point. I ask them to bow and curtsy whenever I mention the fact that the King is parading the streets. There are other points in the tale where the children join in with movements; there are no limits on the number of times the class can get involved. You may have a particular character that you want to associate with a movement. For instance, I use a character called Data Cruncher, and whenever he appears in my stories he does a little pirouette. I ask the class to join in with that, much to their amusement, but again it's a way to get them listening to the tale and anticipating Data Cruncher's arrival.

You could ask the class to split into groups and act out a part of your story, or even make up one of their own. In this case they should select a narrator to tell the tale, and the rest of the group will demonstrate what he or she is saying by delivering the actions. This is a longer exercise which would form part of a main activity.

Voice, movement, posture and expression are the tools of a storyteller's trade. Like magic they can turn an ordinary story into something truly amazing. In classes I call this the 'Story Cake'. The sponge base is the substance of the story, the jam layers are the bridges from beginning, middle and end, and how you present the story is the icing on top. It's the bit that everyone sees and is attracted to. Presentation techniques, if done correctly, will not only give your story credence, they will give your performance confidence. The more you employ these skills in the classroom, the more effective they will become, and if you get your class to join in then you should also see positive results in the areas of speaking and listening.

5 In the Classroom

Introducing your class to storytelling

When I'm working in a class the first thing I do is ask them what they think storytelling is. It's interesting to hear their ideas on the subject. As you would expect, most children believe that storytelling has something to do with reading or writing stories. Some children think it's all about acting, and in a way you are performing your work, but it's a combination of using the right words and movements to create the desired effect. I prefer to think of storytelling as a form of engagement. It's how to use words to deliver a message and connect with your audience. Making it real for them is the most important thing and you have the tools and know-how to do this.

I begin by explaining that in storytelling we make up stories in our heads. We see these stories; we watch them develop like we would watch a film at the cinema. I then ask the class what kind of stories they like to make up. I try to get them thinking in pictures before I even begin my first tale. If, for example, I'm going to tell a story about a king I start by asking them questions. What does a king do? Where does he live? What does he wear? These are prompts to my story which encourage the class to build up a picture of the main character.

I explain that in storytelling we hold the story in our head. We do not write it down, instead the story flows using whatever words we feel necessary at the time. This allows us to be flexible, and use our imaginations. I like to reinforce the idea that in storytelling you can go anywhere you choose to go, there are no limits or barriers.

Of course the best introduction to storytelling is the story. It is much easier to show rather than tell, so begin by setting the scene, asking questions to get your class thinking visually and then present your tale. Watch your audience. Make a mental note of any areas where expressions and eye contact vary. If you think they may be losing interest introduce a sequence or phrase that they can join in with. You are in control. You are taking them on a journey. Five to ten minutes is a good length for a story, anything longer and they will lose interest, anything shorter and they won't have time to become personally involved with the plot and characters.

Once you have delivered your tale, and illustrated the basics of storytelling, you need to devise some class activities. With storytelling the main emphasis in the National Curriculum is on Speaking and Listening, but it can also be used to encourage and improve writing ability, and as an exercise in sharing ideas and working in groups.

Storyboards

Storyboards are an excellent way to introduce children to the world of storytelling because they are a visual aid to telling a story and great fun to produce. Storyboards are similar in pattern and effect to story ladders, the main difference being that a storyboard is made up of pictures and words. A story ladder uses chunks of sentences or phrases to move you on to the next stage of the story. Children find it easier to associate with images in the first instance, although older children might enjoy the challenge of creating a story ladder. I also prefer to use storyboards in class because it gives children who struggle with the written word the opportunity to get involved in an exercise by drawing and talking about their ideas.

You can make your storyboards as easy or as complex as you like (see the illustration of a storyboard on page 38). This is an exercise in using the imagination, and I like to encourage the children to get really colourful and creative. One-page pictures are a simple way to spark tales based on memories, three-page boards split into beginning, middle and end are a good way to get to grips with a basic plot and characters, and the more complicated comic strip-style boards are an excellent way to motivate older children.

I like to use storyboards as a lead-in to storytelling performance work. It gives the class the opportunity to get into groups and really get to grips with the tale. Storyboards can be used as starter or main activities, with outcomes that focus on sharing ideas, communicating in groups and creating coherent plots.

When producing storyboards I ask the class to think of a picture that captures the essence of whichever stage of the story they are focusing on. I then suggest that they write a few key words beneath the picture to help them when it comes to telling their tale. They can also write a sentence for each picture, however I try to steer them away from writing the full narrative as this is an exercise in storytelling and the oral tradition, not reading/writing. If you can get children thinking creatively, experimenting with language and then developing tales in their heads they will have more confidence when it comes to the written word.

Examples of storyboards

Illustrated is a simple beginning/middle/end-type storyboard. Separate sheets of paper can be used for each section of the story. I find this is the best approach for Key Stage 1 and 2 children.

Storyboards can vary in size and include more than three sections depending on the length of the story, and the level of the class. Older children might choose to do either a comic book-style storyboard or get creative with different-shaped storyboards that indicate the twists and turns in a tale.

It's a good idea to prepare worksheets for each group with questions for them to consider. I like to include suggestions for characters, settings and dilemmas (see the example on page 39).

A comic book style storyboard for the tale 'Playing by Numbers'

Title _____

Characters _____

My initial situation _____

The solution _____

1) Briefly describe the section of the story you are going to tell.
   If possible, write your description out in numbered steps.

2) Look at your numbered steps and take any out that don't seem
   like they help you tell the story. Add any in that you feel are missing.

3) Explain how you are going to gather your data, who you are going
   to ask, or where your data is coming from?

4) How you are going to present or analyse your data? What do you
   want it to show?

5) Fill in the chart on the right. For each numbered step of your story,
   fill in a new picture with key words and if possible, a sentence or two.

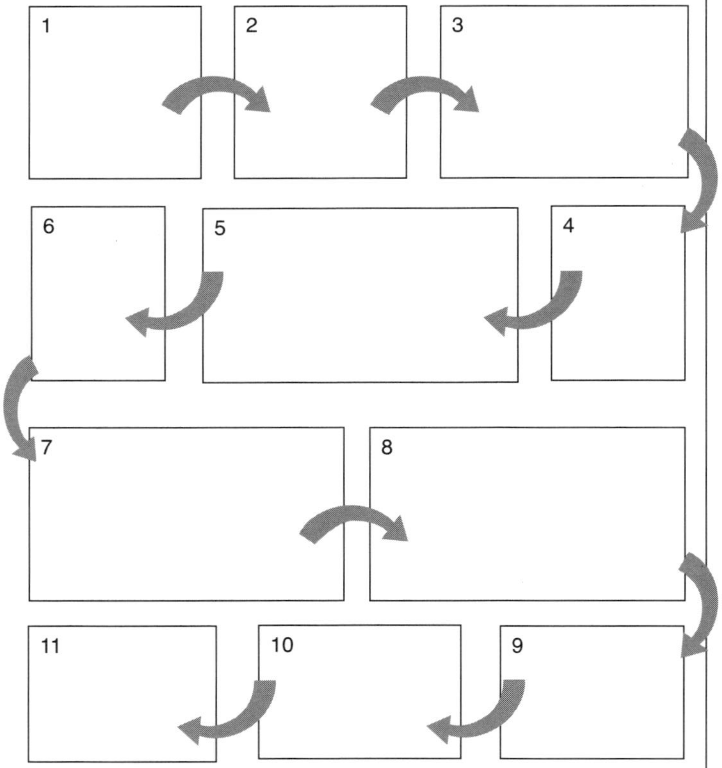

Sample storyboard

Reproduced from *Mathematics Teaching*, 191 Storyboard to accompany: 'Story as a Tool for Learning' by Alison Davies © 2005
www.atm.org.uk/journals/ mathematicsteaching/mt191.html

A simple storyboard for the Tat Rootwhistle tale 'Spot the Difference'

Story worksheet

1) Are any of these characters in your story?

King/Queen	Fairy	Elves
Princess/Prince	Wizard	Vampires
Witch	Demon	Werewolves
Boy/Girl	Giant	Mermaid
Dragon		

2) Are any of these places/things in your story?

Castle	Tee-pee	Mountain
Forest	Tree	Fire
Cave	Tree house	Tower
House	Fountain	Graveyard
Hut	River	Ship

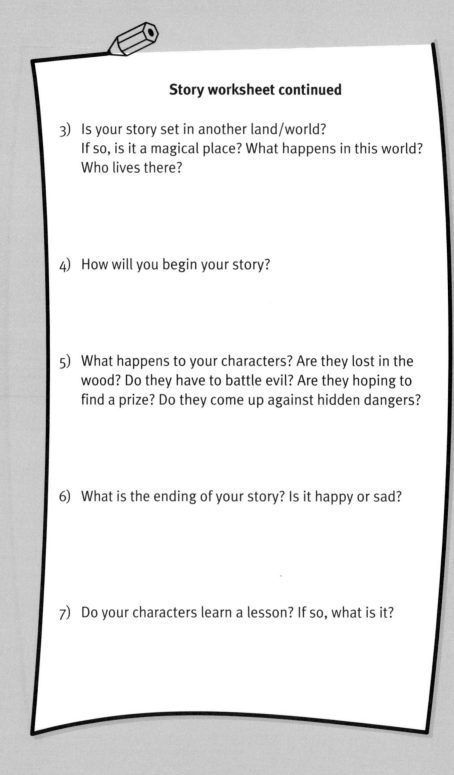

Story worksheet continued

3) Is your story set in another land/world?
   If so, is it a magical place? What happens in this world?
   Who lives there?

4) How will you begin your story?

5) What happens to your characters? Are they lost in the
   wood? Do they have to battle evil? Are they hoping to
   find a prize? Do they come up against hidden dangers?

6) What is the ending of your story? Is it happy or sad?

7) Do your characters learn a lesson? If so, what is it?

Now fill in the box below to help you create your tale.

Outline of story

My story is called ...

The characters in my story are ...

My story is set in ...

Try this in class

I like to provide keywords and sentences to help the class along.

Get a range of brightly coloured sheets of card and cut them to the size of small playing cards, ideal for little fingers. On one colour write several different sentences that might begin a story, on another write sentences that might end a story, and finally on the other colours write action sentences that will move the plot along.

For example, as a beginning sentence you might have:

'There was once a little boy, and he lived in the heart of the forest ...'

A middle sentence might be;

'All of a sudden there was a crashing sound as the trees split in two.'

An ending sentence might be;

'The townsfolk bowed in admiration for the boy had slain the giant.'

Now you can either distribute an equal number of each amongst your groups, or get every member of the group to select a card from each colour group. They can then use your suggestions to help them develop a storyboard.

I carry a story box with me, and in it I include words, sentences, coloured stones, crystals and pictures, anything that might spark ideas. In one of the lesson plans I talk about creating a memory/story box; this can be done individually or as a class. Either way the children find this an exciting exercise, particularly when I show them the story box that I have developed over the years. Each item in my box is a tool that reminds me of a story.

The following are lesson plans that can include storyboard exercises with objectives and outcomes.

Performance/narrative

You will notice that most of the lesson plans reproduced here have some element of performance in them. This is because storytelling deals in the spoken word, and therefore it's essential to get your class speaking and playing with language. I try to steer away from long narrative speeches, and encourage the groups to take it in turns and each take responsibility for a section of the story. It may be that the groups need some direction in this area, and that you have to allocate them parts of the stories to concentrate on. It helps if you give them targets and time frames to accomplish this. I usually give them 20 minutes to begin working on their story, then stop them and find out a little from each group about their story, if it has a title, who is doing which section, how the story begins etc. Then I might give them a further 20 minutes to continue working on it, and again check in after this time and ask them questions. This gets the groups used to the idea of talking about their tale and sharing their ideas with the rest of the class. This means that the final performance is less daunting as they are accustomed to speaking out loud, and know exactly what is expected of them.

Altered perceptions

I often find that children prefer to take on a character from the story, and this should not be discouraged. If they want to tell the story in that character's words then that is perfectly acceptable. It will help both in their characterisation, but also in their ability to empathise with people and situations. This forms the basis of NLP (Neuro-linguistic Programming). You are altering perceptions in order to learn something about a person/situation. You are experiencing the world through someone else's eyes by using your imagination. This is the second perceptual position.

The third perceptual position concerns disconnecting entirely from the situation and viewing it as an outsider. A critic or reviewer might adopt this approach. This is what we do when we are retelling events that happened to us in the past. The way we look at these events is detached, we see ourselves as we were, not as we are.

The first perceptual position is experiencing something firsthand, so if you were telling a tale it would be from your perspective. All of these positions are used in storytelling and are an integral part of the learning and development process.

I encourage pupils to adopt the second perceptual position, particularly if we are doing a session that deals with specific issues such as bullying or peer pressure. I might want them to take one of the Tat Rootwhistle tales and tell it from the perspective of the child who is bullied, or even the bully. I might ask them to explore their feelings about this. Was it difficult thinking from the point of view of the bully, and if so, why did they find it difficult? What is their opinion of bullying? Has telling the story changed their opinion of bullying or bullies? This sort of class activity sparks plenty of discussion.

Sometimes I have pictures of events in stories. These pictures will include characters and I ask the class to imagine what these characters are thinking by looking at their facial expressions. I ask them to draw 'thought bubbles' and fill in what might be going through the character's mind. I encourage them to share this openly in groups or with the rest of the class.

Another valuable exercise would be for one person to imagine that they are one of the characters from the Tat Rootwhistle story, for example Derek the bully in 'Second Chances', and another person to interview Derek. You can do this in pairs, or make it a class exercise and have each pupil taking on different characters and the rest of the class asking them questions. I did this once with a story I'd created about a shepherd boy, especially to celebrate Christmas. The class took it in turns to be the shepherd boy and describe what it was like to see the angel come down and to travel to Bethlehem. They each told a slightly different version of events, and all of them picked different aspects of the character to focus on. As with storytelling, we all see things differently. I may have one picture in my head as I am telling the tale, but the children will also have different pictures in their heads. This is the beauty of storytelling; it is a very personal experience and much can be learnt from this.

Word games

There are very many word games you can incorporate into your storytelling activities, depending on the age and level of your class. Word games are a great ice-breaker and can be used as starter exercises to get the class thinking about language and accustomed to speaking.

The One-Word Game

Tell the class that the aim of this game is to tell a story, but each person is only allowed to say one word and that word must move the story forward. So you might start with 'once' and the next child might say 'upon' and the next one 'a' and on and on it goes until you piece together a story. It's an exercise that should be done at high speed to keep the momentum and the fun going! Some younger children might find it easier to say one sentence rather than one word but the idea is the same – it's very much about ad libbing and stimulating the imagination.

Tripling

This is an exercise for older children, those who have a clear grasp of language and are competent at piecing together stories. The object of the exercise is again to tell a story, but this time the focus is on the language and the meaning of the words chosen. Tripling is something that storytellers use for effect.

It is something I learnt from another storyteller and I have found it immensely helpful in my work.

Each word used in tripling adds something to the picture. It increases the power of the image, to provide maximum impact. For example I have a story, 'The Soul of the City', that I tell to adult audiences where I say, 'The crows they gathered on the Castle Gatehouse, **watching, waiting, counting** the silences'. Here I use tripling to add to the atmosphere and the intention of my words.

With this exercise you get your class to sit in a circle and you start to tell a story. After a minute or two you add in a sentence that uses tripling. So you might say, 'the dog **ran, leapt, bounded** across the field'. Then you move on to the next person. They will continue the tale and include at some point a tripling sentence. The most important thing with this exercise is not to second-guess what is coming up. You cannot know where the story will go, and that is part of the fun and the challenge. You have to think about the story and the language as you are speaking.

Cliffhanger

Again this is a good exercise for older children who are confident with stories. Write a selection of different lines on prompt cards, lines that leave the story hanging in mid air.

So you might have, 'Jenny felt something grab at her shoulder. When she turned around all she could see was ...'

Each child will take it in turns to pick a card and develop the story from this point. They have three minutes to tell this story to the rest of the class. Some children might struggle with this exercise but you can help them by asking questions and getting the rest of the class to join in with suggestions.

In the style of ...

This is another exercise for older, more advanced children.

You pick a selection of well-known fairy tales and write them on different cards, you then write down a selection of character types, for example you might include in this list Witch, King, Ogre, Clown, Fairy, Giant, Pirate etc. Then a class member will pick one card from each group. So they might pick 'The Three Little Pigs' as their story and a Witch as their character. They now have to tell the story of the Three Little Pigs in the style of a witch. So they have to use their voice, facial expression, movement to depict their character whilst telling the tale. You can do famous people, characters from TV etc.

Other class activities

Storytelling can be used in a variety of ways. I often find it is an excellent introduction to subjects that some children might struggle with. For instance, scientific subjects often appear inaccessible to some children, but using storytelling techniques and exercises can offer a different route into the topic and make it enjoyable. An alternative way of looking at things is a breath of fresh air to children who struggle with these subjects. When you tell a story, the class immediately recognises this as fun, as something exciting that they can join in with. This breaks down the barriers instantly. Instead of worrying about the information they are given, they are listening to the tale and engaging with the subject matter. They immediately start to internalise the information and relate to it on a personal level.

My story 'Playing by Numbers' (see page 93) has been used through the Census At School project by several teachers as an introduction to a session on data handling. It can be used in a variety of ways. The teachers might simply choose to read the tale as a way of introducing the topic to the class and encouraging them to think about numbers and data collection. I suggested the following exercise to some of those teachers and the results they had were astounding. After initially reading the story, they asked their class to split into groups and write a similar story whereby the central character had to prove a point or theory by using numbers, just as Sophie did in my original tale. The groups had to think of a plot, and consider how their characters might collect the data they needed to support their theories. The teachers asked them to produce bar charts or graphs as props to the story and as evidence to reinforce the point. In other words, the pupils were engaged in collating and playing with data, they were learning how to use it and quantify it but as part of a larger storytelling activity. This made the subject exciting. It was no longer a routine exercise in maths, but a creative adventure.

Stories can be used in virtually every subject on the curriculum. Imagine studying the Kings and Queens of England through story. Perhaps the class could create and perform tales for each one, relaying the events of the day and what it was like to live in that era. They would have to conduct research to be sure of their facts, but delving into textbooks would become even more enjoyable as they don the time detective's hat ready to tell their tale. They would have to think about costume: how would they move as that particular character, what clothing restrictions did they have in that age? How would they talk? Were they educated? What kind of things would they see?

If you are doing a lesson on different countries and cultures you can enrich the lesson with storytelling. What was is it like to live in Africa? Draw a storyboard to depict a day in the life of a young African boy. Get them to think of key words, how would these key words differ from those of a young British boy? Tell the boy's story from his perspective, or as an outsider. What if they could ride a magic carpet and find themselves in Africa face to face with their character? What adventures might they have? What would they ask that little boy? The potential for stories is amazing, and the more stories the class create and tell, the more confident they will become at expressing themselves. They will find it easy to communicate individually and in groups, they will be motivated in their studies and they will develop a strong creative backbone.

Summary

The lesson plans I have given in this chapter are only examples, and you will find more ideas come to mind as you work through them. Part of the uniqueness of storytelling is its amazing ability to stoke the fires of the imagination. This is because it is an interactive medium whereby one exercise leads to another and so on. As a storyteller you have to learn to release the control on your story, and the outcomes you expect to achieve. In other words, you have to trust that the story will ignite creativity within your class without your dictating what you expect them to gain from the experience. Naturally you will have an idea of what you want them to achieve, but this is not an exercise in command and control. You are delivering information but in a different way, an enjoyable and inspiring way. Storytelling is about personal experience, it's about making it real for the individual, and each person young or old will bring different things to the tale, so the learning will be unique.

The seventeenth-century French philosopher René Descartes, when talking about knowledge and the mind, famously said 'I think therefore I am.' His work was very clear about the separation of mind and body, and that all our focus should be directed on the mind. I prefer John Seely Brown's analogy from his chapter in the book Storytelling in Organizations: 'We participate and therefore we are.' In other words, we can only truly understand something by making it real, by internalising the information and integrating it into a framework. We learn about things by the way we react to them, and this often comes through discussing and sharing with others, by storytelling, in one form or another. As Seely Brown says, 'We are constructing understanding all the time, in conversation or through narratives. We are personalising it through telling stories, and in so doing we are constructing it for ourselves.' He believes that children may receive information in the classroom, but they actually start to construct their own understanding of this information outside of school. By using storytelling in the class you are providing the skills for children to be able to do this. You are enabling them to make sense of what they learn, by participating and personalising it in stories.

Lesson Plan

Lesson: Finding the end of the tale

Learning objectives:
To create a colourful storyboard with key words and sentences.
To look at story development and progression.
To share ideas and communicate in groups, using listening and speaking skills.

Starter: As an introduction the first part of the tale will be delivered by the teacher.	**Pupils** The class will listen to the beginning of the tale and start to think about possible extensions.
	Teacher The teacher will tell the tale, and explain that the children should think about what might happen next. They will encourage pupils to ask questions, and discuss ideas before splitting into groups.
Main: The class will be split into groups (mixed ability or literacy) and given sheets of paper to create their storyboard (beginning, middle and end). Prompts and questions for discussion may also be given to stimulate ideas.	**Pupils** The groups will decide what happens next in the story by answering questions. They will draw a storyboard, and think about key words or sentences to describe what is happening in the pictures.
	Teacher The teacher will encourage each group to come up with ideas for different story endings. They will steer them to a resolution, and ensure that they can describe what is happening in their tale.
Plenary: The groups will display their storyboards and describe what happens in their version of the story.	**Pupils** Each group will tell their version of the story using the storyboard they have created.
	Teacher The teacher will give feedback on each group's story, asking questions wherever possible to encourage the groups to think about the language they use, and how the plot develops.

Outcomes:
All pupils will: Learn about stories and how a plot develops
Most pupils will: Share ideas, through speaking and listening within groups
Some pupils will: Learn how to express themselves using language

Resources: Paper, pencils, crayons

Key words:
Storyboards, characters, language, speaking, listening, sharing.

Cross-Curricular Links:
Personal Social Health Education & Citizenship
Using fables or moral tales asks the groups to think about the lesson behind the story.

Assessment of Learning: Presentation of storyboard and tale. How groups worked together and collated ideas.

Extension Activity: Look at different ways to create atmosphere using language. Search out descriptive words to use for each picture. What type of story are we trying to create? Scary? Exciting? Happy? Sad?

Homework Ideas:
Think of another ending to the story and draw a picture to represent this.
Write the ending of the story using three sentences and/or a selection of key words.

Question Ideas:

What happens to this character in my tale?
Where will my story end? (in a different place?)
Is the ending happy or sad?
Does the character learn anything from the story?
Do I learn anything from this story?

Your Own Notes/Questions:

Notes on Lesson/Evaluation

Lesson Plan

Lesson: Memory Box

Learning Objectives:
To create a colourful memory box (class or individual) and fill it with pictures of memories.
To remember events that have passed and what was good or bad about them and share this.
To describe these memories with the help of a picture and keywords.

Starter:	Pupils	Teacher
A memory box should be created and decorated. This box will be used to store pictures of memories and keywords.	The class will split into groups to create their memory box. A basic shoebox will suffice.	The teacher will introduce the memory box and get the children to decorate it. The teacher will encourage the class to think about the kind of things they want to put inside.

Main:	Pupils	Teacher
The class will draw pictures of memories and write key words on the back of their drawings.	The pupils will come up with one or two memories, and draw a picture to represent what happened. They will then write a handful of key words on the back of their drawing to help them describe it.	The teacher will encourage the class to think about events that happened and how they would describe them. What language will they use? Are these happy or sad memories? What key words sum up the point of the story?

Plenary:	Pupils	Teacher
The pictures will be placed in the box, and the teacher will draw them out one by one so that each child can share his or her memory with the rest of the class.	The pupils will take it in turns, in pairs to tell each other their memory. They will then tell their memory to the rest of the class.	The teacher will facilitate the drawing out of memories using pictures and keywords.

Outcomes:

All pupils will:	Think of a memory and draw a picture to describe it.
Most pupils will:	Use key words to describe their memories, and share these memories with friends/class.
Some pupils will:	Express themselves using fluent language, and turn their memories into stories.

Resources: Paper, pencils, crayons, box for decoration

Key words:	Cross-Curricular Links:
Memories, events, pictures, words, language, speaking, listening, sharing, stories	Personal Social Health Education & Citizenship

Assessment of Learning: Presentation of memory box, and memories, how these memories are told in small groups and to the rest of the class.

Extension Activity: Pick out someone else's picture/memory from the box, and try to tell their tale using the picture and key words. How different is it from their story? What language did you use?

Homework Ideas: Find another memory (happy/sad/exciting/funny) and draw a picture to represent this with key words. How would you tell this to your classmates?

Question Ideas:

What makes a memory?
Is your memory, happy/sad/exciting/funny/scary?
What words would you use to describe how it made you feel?
How would you begin to tell your memory to someone else?
What picture would you use to sum up what happened to you?

Your Own Notes/Questions:

Classifying words (key)

Feelings – Activity – Action – People – Time – Place

Notes on Lesson/Evaluation

Lesson Plan

Lesson: Create a story/storyboard

Learning Objectives:
To produce a story using prompt cards and sentences and/or a story wizard.
To create a storyboard to illustrate the story, with key words.
To tell the story to the rest of the class.

Starter: A short storytelling session with the class discussing what storytelling is, and what kind of stories they might like to create.	**Pupils** The pupils will listen and join in with the storytelling session. They will discuss what storytelling is, and how a story is formed. They will also think about the type of characters they might have in their story, and the setting.	**Teacher** The teacher will lead the storytelling session. They will encourage the pupils to think about storytelling. They may use the board to list hints and tips, and/or produce an outline of the storyboard for the class to follow in their groups. The teacher will explain how to use the prompt cards and/or story wizard.
Main: The class will split into groups (mixed or literacy) and they will use the prompt cards and/or story wizard to develop their story. They will draw a storyboard, and list key words.	**Pupils** The pupils will use either the prompt cards or the story wizard to come up with a framework for their story. They will think about characters, and themes and they will begin to draw their storyboard. They will also think about key words for their tale.	**Teacher** The teacher will assist the groups in creating a framework for the story. They will encourage them to think about key words and language as well as characters, setting and plot.
Plenary: The groups will spend an alloted time rehearsing their story. Ideally each member will take a section of the tale and tell it. They will use only the pictures and the key words, although they may want to create props to help them with their final presentation.	**Pupils** The pupils will each take a section of the story that they will tell. They will think about the words they might use, and how they might describe what is happening and the characters. They will spend time practising this in their groups.	**Teacher** The teacher will help the groups rehearse their tale, giving them feedback and making sure that they are all involved in the presentation. At the end of the lesson each group will be given the chance to perform their piece.

Outcomes:

All pupils will: Create a storyboard using the prompt cards or the story wizard.
Most pupils will: Take a section of the story and tell it, using key words.
Some pupils will: Act out the story, thinking about language, expression and movement (getting under the character's skin).

Resources: Paper, pencils, crayons

Key words: Stories, plot, characters, themes, lessons, language, action, description, emotion, storyboards.	**Cross-Curricular Links:**

Assessment of Learning: Through the production of storyboards, the presentation of the story, the way the groups worked together and shared the tasks. Personal involvement in the tale.

Extension Activity: In groups – practise the tale and create suitable props for the story. Is it something you could share with other classes/year groups/parents/teachers? Individually use the story wizard/prompt cards to create your own story.

Homework Ideas: Get the children to take a character from their story and write a paragraph about them, who they are, where they live, what they do, likes/dislikes etc.

Question Ideas:

What is storytelling?
What kind of characters are there in my story?
Who is my favourite character?
Why do I like this character?
What might they live?
What might they do?
How does this character fit into my story?
How does my story end?
What words best describe the character I like the best?
Are there any characters I don't like? Why is this?

Your Own Notes/Questions:

Notes on Lesson/Evaluation

Lesson Plan

52

Lesson: Tell My Story (character exercise)		Question Ideas:

Learning Objectives:
To produce a story from the perspective of another character or an inanimate object.
To identify different character traits and empathise with them.
To look at the story from another perspective.
To learn about characterisation.

Question Ideas:
List some of the other characters in the story.
Are there any objects that speak?
Do they have a name?
What do they do? Are they magical?
What would it be like to be them?
How do they move, speak, eat etc.?
Would you like to be a tree?
What do you think you might notice if you were a tree?
How would you feel? Tall and strong, or old and shaky?
Would you swap places with any of the characters in the story?
If so, would you do things differently?
What kind of magical powers would you like?
What kind of magical powers does your character have?
Would you choose your character as a friend?
What is happening in your character's life and what is their story?

Starter:
The class will begin with some storytelling, for example one of the Tat Rootwhistle tales in which the class can interact and get involved. They will discuss the other characters in the story, as well as inanimate objects that might be alive given the magical context of the tale. What would these characters and/or objects see or feel? How involved are they in the tale?

Pupils
The pupils become involved in the storytelling and discuss other characters and the role they play in the story.

Teacher
The teacher uses the Tat Rootwhistle tale to engage with the class and get them thinking about characters (people/animals or objects). How does the story look from their perspective? What part do they play in it?

Main:
The class (either in groups or individually) will pick a character and/or object from the tale and make up it's story. Worksheets or direction on the board may be given to stimulate ideas.

Pupils
The pupils pick a character from the Tat Rootwhistle story, and give this character a personality. They might want to draw their character and list its attributes.

Teacher
The teacher will help the class to create characters, asking questions in order to build up a picture. If the character is an object the teacher will encourage the class to think of the kind of words that object might use, how it would talk/move. For example, what would the voice of a tree sound like?

Plenary:
The class share their ideas in pairs or with the rest of the class.

Pupils
The pupils will share their characters with the rest of the class using pictures and stories to describe who they are and how they live.

Teacher
The teacher will give feedback on the characters created and the kind of stories that they may have. Is there potential for a new story that the class could create together using these new characters and a different setting?

Your Own Notes/Questions:

Review key vocab and put new words on board

Outcomes:
All Pupils Will: Choose/create a character and be able to describe what it looks like.
Most Pupils Will: Be able to describe what their characters thinks/feels/likes.
Some Pupils Will: Be able to empathise with their character and see the story from their perspective.

Resources: Paper, pencils, crayons, list of possible characters

Key words: characters, thoughts, feelings, likes, dislikes, voice, movement, colour, picture, appearance	**Cross-Curricular Links:**

Assessment of Learning: Through the creation of a character; the ability to describe the character and their story.

Extension Activity: Get the children to imagine a conversation with their character. What would happen if they met? What would they ask their character? Get them to write down the conversation. This might take the form of an interview.

Homework Ideas: The children should describe a day in the life of their character. What might they eat for breakfast? Do they go to school, if so, what do they study? Where is their school? What do they do for fun? Who is their best friend? Do they have any pets? Do they have TV?

Notes on Lesson/Evaluation:

Lesson Plan

Lesson: Playing by Numbers (Data Handling Story Exercise)		Question Ideas:
Learning Objectives: To understand the importance of gathering data to solve a problem To create a story focusing on aspects of data handling To collect data to answer an hypothesis To display data in a chart or diagram as part of the storyboarding exercise		How does Master Data Cruncher help Sophie? What is data? How is it used in the story? How would Sophie have collected her data? How would she have presented it, and why? Where might you use data? Is it better to list numbers or produce a chart? Do you think data is important? Do you like working with numbers?
Starter: The class will listen to 'Playing by Numbers'. A discussion will follow about the importance of collecting data, and the different ways that this can be done.	**Teacher** The teacher will use the tale as a way to introduce data handling. They will instigate a discussion on the importance of data, using examples on the board, and examples taken from the story.	Your Own Notes/Questions:
	Pupils The pupils will listen to the story and discuss the purpose of data handling. They will discuss ways in which data can be collected and presented (bar charts, graphs, diagrams, lists) H D Cycle!	
Main: The class will split into groups and begin working on a similar tale, or even the same story if they wish. They will consider how Sophie gathered her data, and they will carry out similar tasks to produce data which can then be presented in charts, diagrams or graphs. Examples for possible data collection may be given on a worksheet from the teacher. They will then include this in their own story, or as part of their storyboard presentation.	**Teacher** The teacher will encourage the class to think about similar situations. They will provide worksheets with suggestions and questions to stimulate ideas. The teacher will help the groups to collate the data and put it in a presentable format. The data element should be a key part of the tale.	
	Pupils The pupils will split into groups and discuss how they would collect data. They will think about similar situations where data might be needed to prove a point, and they will work a story around this. As part of the story/storyboard presentation they will produce diagrams/graphs and charts to show how they would handle the data.	
Plenary: The group will present their story and data to the rest of the class.	**Teacher** The teacher will give feedback on the way the data has been used in the story. Does it provide evidence and is it clear and understandable?	
	Pupils The pupils will present their tale including data to the class. They will explain the importance of the data and why they chose to present it in this format.	

Outcomes:
All pupils will: Understand the importance of data handling and recognise the different ways to present data.
Most pupils will: Be able to think of examples where data handling would help to prove a theory and be able to build a story around this.
Some pupils will: Be able to present the data in a clear and concise manner and explain why they have done this.

Resources: Paper, pencils, graph paper, examples of charts, worksheets

Key words: Evidence, data, collection, numbers, theories, charts, graphs, lesson, story.	Cross-Curricular Links:

Prior Knowledge: The concept of data handling in mathematics.

Assessment of Learning: Through the data collected and the way it is presented, how the children interact and understand why they need data to support a theory and as part of their story.

Extension Activity: Get the children to think of another way to present the same data – would it be easier to understand in a bar chart? What about a graph? Or could they simply list the figures? What difference does this make to those viewing the data for the first time?

Homework Ideas: Take the character Data Cruncher and get the children to create another story for him. Where does he live? What is the land of numbers like? Could they include some simple maths in the story? Perhaps they visit Data Cruncher and ask him to help them learn their times tables etc.

Notes on Lesson/Evaluation

6 Happily Ever After

Ideas for extension activities and homework

Storytelling does not stop in the classroom. Storytelling is all around us. When children go home they probably launch into a number of different stories … 'Mum guess what happened today in the playground' or 'We did this in class today ….' They are telling stories constantly. By using this oral tradition in the classroom we are teaching children to recognise the use of stories and to improve their verbal communication skills. This learning programme continues when they finish the school day, and as they progress through life. We all appreciate a good story and it's a way of creating a common experience. Storytelling helps to improve our social interaction skills.

Although some of the homework exercises I have suggested in the lesson plans are individual activities where the child creates a storyboard, or character, the actual act of storytelling continues. I try to encourage children to share the stories they have created with parents and carers and friends. I also ask them to listen to other people's stories. I believe listening is equally important in storytelling, and one way to improve this skill is to get the children to create a storybox (the memory box is a similar idea and can also be used). They can keep this box at home or at school and use it specifically to gather tales that they have heard.

So as part of a homework activity I would ask them to collect a tale from someone in their family, to listen to that tale and then draw a picture (or pictures) to represent what happened, and also write key words, and then place this in their storybox. We would then have a storytelling session at some point in class where the children get the chance to tell the tales they have collected. The stories can be very simple, it depends on the age group, but I would suggest giving them key questions or topics to help them find their tale.

These topics might be:

Try this in class

Family holiday

1 Where did you go on holiday when you were my age?

2 What did you do whilst you were there?

3 What was your favourite holiday and why?

4 Did anything funny happen whilst you were away?

5 Did you make new friends?

6 What kind of adventures did you have?

You could then ask the child to draw comparisons between family holidays in the past and present. Are there any clear differences in destination and habits? This is a good exercise in examining social history.

SCHOOL

1 Where did you live when you were my age, and what was that like?

2 What was school like?

3 Did you have a favourite subject?

4 Can you remember any of your teachers and what were they like?

5 What kind of games did you play in the playground?

HOBBIES

1 What did you like doing when you were my age?

2 Where did you go to play?

3 Did you like sport/reading/playing games etc.?

4 Did you watch television?

5 What were your friends like?

Some schools I have visited have arranged a special storytelling performance session. The school has invited family and friends to come in for the afternoon and be a part of this. The classes have split into groups and performed some of their stories; in some cases individuals have told stories from their memory box. Then the families and friends have been invited to tell tales and memories to the groups. This exchange of tales is essentially what storytelling is all about; different generations of people sharing their thoughts, ideas and feelings. It is a useful exercise for the class as it builds on speaking and listening skills, helps in personal development and social interaction, and it's fun.

This kind of exercise, whether carried out by individuals at home gathering tales or in a show-and-tell classroom environment, can be used to complement a variety of subjects. The obvious choice might be history, and examining how things were in the past through sharing stories. A similar exercise might work in geography: think of using stories about a place, asking friends/family what their experience of that place was, and what they remember about the landscape.

Why not bring in a piece of sandstone, a crystal or even a fossil and after a starter session explaining what it is, ask the children to tell its story. Where does it live, what does it do there, what has it seen and what was it used for? These are all alternative ways of understanding the nature of things, and can instigate some wonderful discussions.

You might feel confident enough to make up a story about your artefact. This might be easier and a more exciting introduction to a topic than trying to regurgitate facts for your class.

I once created a story based upon a cave beneath the castle wall in Nottingham. The cave is part of an inn, which some consider to be the oldest inn in the UK. I wanted to tell the history of the place, of the Crusaders who stopped by on their way to war in the Holy Land, so I told the story as if I was the rock, living and breathing and remembering the past. This not only made my story personal, but it meant I gave a confident delivery of the facts from a new perspective. It was also a way to hint at some of the ghostly goings on associated with the place, because I gave the place a life of its own.

Music is another subject that storytelling complements. Children at whatever age can appreciate this. Play them a piece of music in class and ask them to think about how the music makes them feel. What does it remind them of? Are they thinking of a particular place, or person? Does it make them feel excited, scared, happy, sad? If they were to draw a picture to represent that piece of music what would it be? What would the story be behind the picture? As homework ask them to pick a piece of music and think about the story behind this. They might want to use a piece of music as part of their storytelling performance work, or maybe they have a piece of music they would like to put in their memory box? If so ask them why? What tales spring to mind when they hear this music? Storytelling uses all the senses, because as the storyteller you place yourself in the tale in order to experience it and make that experience real for others. It is only when you can truly relate to something that you begin to understand it, therefore if you use stories as a way of connecting with music, history, geography, science or mathematics you are opening the gateway for this relationship to occur. This also works when dealing with particular issues or subjects that might be difficult to cover.

The stories included in this book touch on a variety of subjects that are important to children – bullying, peer pressure, obesity, cultural diversity, disability etc. They are moral tales, and I have written them with specific messages in mind. They can be used as an introduction to the topic and further discussion. They can be used as part of a storytelling lesson plan. They should be used as a starting point for further stories, and in that way the children will be able to identify with what is going on. The minute they put themselves in the tale everything changes. Children who otherwise struggle with language and expressing themselves will find it easier to do so in a story that has no limitations. They are not writing, so they do not have to struggle with words, they are simply seeing, experiencing and expressing this.

For example, the story about obesity might provide the perfect springboard for homework on food groups and healthy eating. After listening to the story, discussing Pagan's problem, and then if possible creating their own stories around this subject, the children will have explored the value of healthy eating and exercise. This is the ideal opportunity for them to look at food groups, and to evaluate what they eat on a regular basis. You might want to devise a questionnaire for them to complete, and then they could put the information they collect into a bar chart or graph. What started out as a simple storytelling activity has developed into food science, health and ultimately a mathematics or statistics lesson.

The Tat Rootwhistle story included in Part Two about the ladybird with only one spot is a tale about being different and what that means. It's about accepting who you are and embracing your differences. Why not tell this story to your class and ask them to finish it? I wonder how different their endings might be to the one in the book. Do they help the ladybird to change, or do they help him find happiness as he is? What do they want to happen, and what do they think should happen? Through discussion and storytelling they learn that being different is not a bad thing, and that we are all unique.

As a homework or extension activity help your class to discover more differences in insects. Why not get them to list different types of beetles, or spiders? Invite them to explore their garden or local park: how many different insects can they see and what are they? What is the world like from the insects' perspective? Perhaps they could create a new story taking an insect from their back garden or local park and giving it a character. Ask them to think about this insect: what does it look like, where does it live, what does it eat? You can do exactly the same thing with trees, plants or flowers, the options are endless. Immediately you have taken a journey from storytelling to the important lesson of acceptance (of ourselves and others) into natural history and the creatures that we share the earth with; all different, but all with a unique beauty.

I hope these chapters have given you an insight into the wonderful world of storytelling and how beneficial it can be in teaching and learning. I hope I have given you food for thought, and inspired you to have a go. There is no right or wrong way; there is only your way, as the storyteller. You can use stories to engage, educate and entertain. You can use them as a channel of information, or as a tool for healing and understanding. Most of all they should be used to open the doors of creativity and add colour and texture to life.

Children are excellent storytellers; they do not sense some of the constraints of society that we as adults put upon ourselves. They have vivid imaginations, and given the right environment and encouragement, they are not afraid to use them!

Part Two Tales for Telling

Part Two of this book comprises of a series of stories for you to use, some of which I have mentioned previously. These stories have all been used in classroom situations. Some of the stories have been condensed at the time, and often when I tell them I use different words from these written here or I edit them as I see fit. My hope is that you will be able to pick and choose stories to illustrate your point. Play around with them, chop out bits you don't like and try to create bits of your own. Recognise different styles and discover what works for you. Use these stories as springboards into creating your own tales and introducing storytelling to your class.

Practise learning these tales with the story ladder technique. Take some of the characters and work on performance and delivery: how will you distinguish between the characters, how would they speak and move? Think about the meaning of each tale: what is the message of the story and how can you get this across to your audience? In some cases the stories can be used to introduce discussion topics such as bullying, peer pressure, obesity, disabilities etc. How might you do this with these tales? Is there an opportunity for groups to work on a storyboarding exercise, or would it be more appropriate for individuals to produce pictures for a memory box?

In other cases you might want to use the stories to introduce another subject like mathematics or religion or natural history. If the stories don't fit with what you had in mind, then have a go at producing your own, and just borrow some of the characters. Perhaps the stories remind you of something that happened in the past, something you can use with your class. Either way, read them, digest them, use the bits you want, discard those you don't and, remember, practise.

The King's Cloak –
a traditional tale

The following story, so far as I know, is traditional; it was passed on by the oral tradition and told to me by another storyteller who has changed elements of the tale to suit his needs. I also took the tale and adapted it to fit with the requirements of my storytelling sessions. With each telling the tale becomes something new, something quite detached from the original story. A little like Chinese whispers, the story has developed over the years and taken on unique properties from each storyteller. Here is my version, with pointers on how it can be used in the classroom. I think it illustrates exactly what storytelling is. Not only is it an excellent tool for engaging with the class, but it also stimulates discussion about the power of stories and how we use them today.

Before beginning this tale, I always ask the class if they can describe what a king might look like. I ask them to picture a king in their mind and tell me what he might wear, where he lives, how he might act etc. This gets them thinking along the right lines, so already we are starting to form a communal landscape.

There was once a King, a lot like the Kings that you have described. He was a very grand man. He lived in a vast kingdom of a thousand valleys and he had many servants. This King was so rich he could have bought the earth as it is today three times over, but do you know what he preferred to spend his wealth upon?

An opportunity for the children to guess!

He loved to spend money on clothes. Oh yes, he had clothes for every occasion, clothes that not only filled wardrobes they filled entire rooms. You name it, the King had an outfit for everything! And he was so incredibly vain. He loved nothing more than to strut up and down in front of the royal mirror and admire his reflection. Sticking out his belly, he would lovingly pose and smile at what he saw. So you can imagine that to be the King's Tailor was a very difficult job indeed, and if you didn't get the outfit quite right, it was off with your head! Many a tailor came to a gruesome end at the hands of the King's arrogance.

Now the King's latest tailor was a young and clever lad who soon realised how to keep the King happy. All he had to do was to convince him that whatever he made was truly special and something the King could not find anywhere else. He also realised that because of the King's vanity, he would be able to have some fun, and make him look totally ridiculous.

One day he happened to spot the King's maid servant taking some smelly old kitchen rags to the royal dustbin. Now let me explain, these kitchen rags were the smelliest, filthiest, stinkiest kitchen rags you've even seen, and she held them aloft between two fingers whilst pinching her nose. Just as she was about to drop the rags into the dustbin the Tailor stepped forward.

'Hold on, hold on,' he said. 'Don't be throwing that away, I could do something with that!'

And he grabbed the stinky, smelly kitchen rags and whisked them away to his tower room. There he worked through the night, cutting, sewing and weaving. He worked so hard he thought his fingers might wear to the bone. When at last he had done, guess what he had made for the King to wear …

An opportunity for the children to join in and guess what the Tailor has made.

The Tailor made a cloak for the King to wear. Now when he presented this cloak to the King he wasn't too sure about it, after all, the material still smelt terrible. But the Tailor explained that this material was made from the tears of fairies and so had a very special quality to it that gave it a somewhat different scent. The King was very pleased with this indeed. A cloak made from fairies' tears, how wonderful! He put it on immediately and admired his reflection. He loved the way the fabric floated about his person. In fact he loved it so much that he spent the day walking about his kingdom so that all of the people could admire him. Naturally the people stopped and stared, they bowed and they curtsied, and they said, 'Oh sir, oh your majesty, don't you look a dandy!'

This is an opportunity for the children to join in and repeat a phrase. You can also get them to act out the bowing and the curtsying.

Well the king, he loved that cloak so much that he wore it all the time, day in day out, week in week out. He wore it for what seemed like a year and a day

until the cloak no longer hung like a veil. It was worn and tatty and even more smelly than before. There was nothing else for it, he gave it to the maid servant to put it in the royal dustbins. But guess who happened to be walking by at the time? The Tailor. And what do you think he said?

'Hold on, hold on. Don't be throwing that away, I could do something with that!'

So the Tailor took the old and ragged cloak and he whisked it away to his tower room and he worked into the night, cutting, sewing and weaving. He got rid of reams of material until eventually, he made for the king … what do you think he made for the King?

Another opportunity for the children to guess.

He made a waistcoat, and once more the king was not too sure when he saw the waistcoat, but the Tailor convinced him that it was magical.

'Made from dragons' wings,' he said with a sly whisper, 'Oh yes, this is truly special your majesty!'

So the king put on the waistcoat and he admired his reflection. It did make him feel very brave, just like he had the heart of a dragon. He liked the waistcoat so much that he went out onto the city streets and paraded up and down with his belly sticking out. And the people they stopped and they stared, they bowed and they curtsied and they said,

'Oh sir, oh your majesty, don't you look a dandy!'

Well the King simply loved this attention, so he decided to wear the waistcoat all of the time. He wore it day in day out, week in week out, in fact he wore it so much that it began to get torn and tatty, and in the end he just had to take it off. So he sent for the maid servant and asked her to take the rather smelly piece of cloth to the royal dustbins. But guess who happened to be walking by …

And what do you think he said?

He said, 'Hold on, hold on. Don't be throwing that away, I could do something with that!'

By this stage the children will be repeating this phrase.

So he took the smelly old waistcoat and he whisked it up into his tower room and he worked into the night, cutting, sewing and weaving. He worked so hard that he almost worked his fingers to the bone. Now guess what he came up with for the King to wear this time?

I usually repeat this guessing game five or six times and I use the following items of clothing, but this is flexible and you can choose whatever you like, as long as the items of clothing reduce in size to reflect the Tailor's work:

Vest

Hat

Scarf

Bow tie

Button

I follow the same pattern of events with the King showing off his garments and the people responding in awe, until eventually the clothes wear out and they are sent to the royal dustbins to be recycled by the Tailor into something new. Then the Tailor makes the final item for the King, which in my case is a button. This is how the story proceeds from here.

The Tailor made a tiny fabric button for the King to wear. Now this button was very special and looked like a medal, and so the King wore it on his collar with pride. He paraded around the kingdom with his head held high so that everyone could admire it. And of course the people they stopped and stared and bowed and curtsied, and they said,

'Oh sir, oh your majesty, don't you look a dandy!'

So the King felt even more important than before. He loved wearing that button, he thought it was fantastic. So he wore it all the time. He wore it day in day out, week in week out, he wore it so much that it soon began looking ragged. It was dirty and tatty and when he took it off, all that was left were a couple of strands of cotton. So he gave these two tiny strands of cotton to the maid servant and told her to take them to the royal dustbins, but guess who happened to be wandering by ...

Yes, that's right, it was the King's Tailor, and when he saw what the maid had in her hands he cried out,

'Hold on, hold on. Don't be throwing that away. I could do something with that!'

He picked up the strands of cotton and held them for a moment. There was really nothing left of the material that had once been smelly kitchen rags. What on earth could he do with it now? Then he smiled. He knew exactly what he would do with these cotton strands.

That night he wove those two strands into his hair, he packed his bags and he left the kingdom. He spent his days wandering from place to place, and instead of weaving clothes for a living, he wove tales; wonderful magical tales that he told for the price of his supper and a warm comfy bed for the night. He became a travelling storyteller and he captivated audiences with his enchanting tales. As the years passed his hair grew long and thick and so did the two cotton strands and whenever anyone asked him about the colourful threads braided in his hair he began to tell them his favourite tale, the one about the King who wore nothing but smelly old kitchen rags for days on end. Of course no one ever believed the story to be real, and maybe it had changed a bit, like the young Tailor, over the years. For the beauty of tales is that they grow just like the threads in the Tailor's hair. They become something new and colourful, something timeless.

Spot the Difference – a Tat Rootwhistle tale

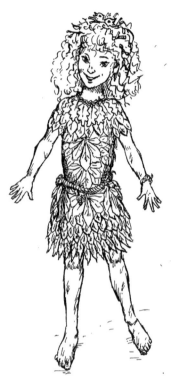

I have added some tips on how and when to involve your class in the telling of this tale. In a place beyond time and space there exists a forest, but this is no ordinary forest. This is the First Forest and it is enchanted. It's a place where the magic runs deep, and the trees stretch up to the heavens, their branches brushing the stars; a place where the grass is a carpet of gold and the flowers are all the colours of the rainbow. And the air smells sweet, of honey and chocolate and all things good. As for the animals, they talk and you and I can understand them. And in this place of a thousand dreams there lives a girl, a wild girl with a thatch of raspberry-coloured hair. She spends her days swinging through the trees, and helping people, because that's what she likes to do, and her name is Tat, Tat Rootwhistle.

Also in this place there lives a tiny ladybird, but he is very sad because he is different.

At this point ask the class to describe a ladybird, what is it that all ladybirds have?

All the other ladybirds that live in the Forest have lots of spots but he only has one; just a single black spot upon his back.

One day this ladybird was sitting on a tree and feeling very sorry for himself. He began to tap his legs upon the bark in frustration. Rat-a-tat-tat, the sound went.

Get the class to join in with you, doing the actions and the sounds of the ladybird on the tree.

Rat-a-tat-tat, over and over, until eventually there was a gust of wind above his head, and there hanging from the branch was small girl with wild, clumpy hair.

'You called?' said the girl.

'Did I?' asked the ladybird, his heart was heavy.

'You called my name, Tat, and now I'm here, and it looks like you could do with some help. Whatever is the matter?'

So the ladybird began to tell his story. He told Tat how all the other ladybirds in the forest would stare at him because he only had one spot. How lonely he felt, and how he longed to be the same as everyone else.

'I'd do anything to have more spots,' he sighed.

Tat looked thoughtful, and then suddenly her eyes lit up and she smiled.

'I know someone who might be able to help. Come with me.'

She held out her hand and the ladybird hopped upon her palm.

Together they flew through the trees, swinging from branch to branch. The breeze whistled above their heads, and the sunlight warmed them.

They came to a clearing and there stood a thatched cottage. Spirals of smoke curled from the chimney.

'Who lives here?' asked the ladybird.

'A witch.'

'A witch? I don't like the sound of that!'

Tat grinned, 'No silly, she's a good witch and she's going to help you find more spots.'

With that, Tat sprang to the ground and tapped on the door. The lady that met them was small and grey with soft features and kindly eyes. Tat explained the ladybird's unhappiness and asked if there was anything the Witch could do to ease his plight.

'Why of course there is, my dear. We'll cast a spell and see if we can get you some more spots.'

The ladybird jumped up and down in excitement.

'At last, I'm not going to be different any more!'

The Witch pulled out a large black cooking pot and began to gather ingredients.

Ask the class what the Witch might put in her cooking pot.

'A little of this, and a little of that ...' she muttered as she dropped things into the pot. The liquid inside began to bubble and turn the strangest shade of purple. On and on she stirred and then with a satisfied smile she picked up a small acorn cup and filled it with the mixture.

'Drink this,' she said to the ladybird.

Within seconds the ladybird could feel the warm liquid in his stomach. His eyelids felt like lead and his head began to spin. What was happening? He looked at Tat and then at the Witch, and then his eyes closed and he dropped into a deep sleep. When he awoke he was back on the very same tree from earlier. He peered down into the small brook beneath the tree. He could see himself in the sparkling water. He squinted and strained until he had a good view but there was still only one spot upon his back.

'I don't believe it! The spell didn't work!' he cried.

How could it not work? He tapped his legs upon the bark in frustration. Rat-a-tat-tat, it went, rat-a-tat-tat, over and over the sound rang through the trees.

Again get the class to join in repeating the phrase and the actions.

Until eventually there was a sharp, biting breeze above his head, and there appeared Tat.

'It didn't work,' he sighed. 'The spell didn't work and now I'm just as different as always. I'm never going to get any more spots.'

Tat shook her head, 'You can't give up yet.'

She looked at the ladybird for the longest time and then she smiled.

'I have it, I have the answer! I know someone who can help.'

With that she held out her hand again and the ladybird hopped upon her palm. They travelled through the trees even faster than before. Branches soared past and the air bristled against their cheeks. Eventually they came to another clearing, and there in the space was the strangest thing the ladybird had ever seen.

'What is that?' he asked, pointing to what looked like a large triangular tent with patterns and drawings upon it.

'That's a tee-pee,' said Tat. 'It's where the Medicine Man of the Forest lives. He's very wise. I'm sure he'll be able to help you.'

Sure enough the man that emerged from the tent looked very wise indeed. He had long black hair worn in two plaits which were decorated with braids and shells. He had coffee-coloured skin and large, shiny, beetle eyes. He looked at the ladybird for the longest time and then he began to play his drum.

His fingers tapped against the smooth skin, rat-a-tat-tat, rat-a-tat-tat …

Then he got this powerful look in his eyes, and he turned to the ladybird.

'Little friend,' he said, 'for you to find the happiness you seek you must travel to the very centre of the First Forest and find the Dreaming Tree. It is the tallest, widest tree in the forest, and its bark shines silver under the moon. You must spend one night sleeping beneath its branches and when you wake you will find what you are looking for.'

'Wow,' said the ladybird, 'so if I find this tree, then I'll get my spots and at last I'll be happy!'

They thanked the Medicine Man and once more began their journey through the Forest, taking it branch by branch, hopping and dancing through the tree tops. On and on they went, for what seemed like hours, and slowly the sun began to set and the sky became a blanket of darkness. Stars peppered the heavens, beautiful shimmering stars that caught the eye, and then at last they saw it; the tallest, widest tree in the forest, with bark that shone silver under the moon. The ladybird didn't waste any time. He jumped from Tat's palm and landed on the ground beneath the tree. It felt soft and moist as he lay down and within seconds he was asleep. This time when he slept he dreamed, and it was the strangest dream he'd ever had because it felt so real.

He was still in the First Forest and he was surrounded by hundreds and thousands of ladybirds, and they all had more spots than him, twos and threes and even fours. They were looking at him, really staring and then he realised something. They all looked exactly the same. It was hard to tell the difference between any of them. Instead of laughing at him there was something else in their eyes, a glint of admiration and awe. Yes they were looking at him because he was different, but they were admiring him! They were envious because he stood out, and that made him feel very special indeed. So special that he began to smile, and that smile warmed him from top to bottom.

When the little ladybird awoke he was back sitting on the same tree as he had been the previous day, but things were different. He didn't have any more spots, but that didn't matter because he was happy, really truly happy. He realised that being different was a good thing. He was special, unique; there was no one in the world like him. How fantastic was that? Quickly he began tapping his legs on the tree.

Another opportunity for the class to repeat the phrase.

Rat-a-tat-tat, rat-a-tat-tat, and when at last she appeared in a flurry of leaves, he squealed with excitement.

'I'm happy, I'm really happy!'

Tat wriggled her nose and looked confused.

'But I don't understand, you've still only got one spot. The night under the Dreaming Tree didn't help.'

'I know,' the Ladybird smiled, 'and I'm glad because I've learnt something important. I like being different. It's a good thing. I'm special you see.'

'Well I could have told you that,' grinned Tat.

So it was that the little ladybird lived a very happy life in the First Forest, and the fact that he only had one spot didn't worry him any more. He liked to stand out from the crowd.

As for Tat, she carried on her merry ways, spending her days swinging through the trees, and helping where she could, because that's what Tat does. She makes things better, in the First Forest, and in a million other places too.

Second Chances –
a Tat Rootwhistle tale

Beyond the forests of time, somewhere between the city's sprawling streets, lives a girl. This is no ordinary girl. With spindly cricket legs, and a raspberry thatch of hair, she's wild as wild can be. In the day she runs with the wind. Her friends are the reedy grasses that tickle and cling to raggedy clothes. At night she's a feral child, climbing the highest trees, swinging from crooked branch to branch. She goes by the name Tat Rootwhistle, but there are those with other names for her. The spirits from the first world, the great mother earth, they protect her, for she is their daughter. And she knows about the world today, but prefers to watch from her tiny corner of reality. It's easier that way, like becoming someone else for a while. Occasionally she'll stray into real-time bringing the magic of the forest with her. But more often it's the real time that seeks her out, and is changed forever by their meeting.

Tommy liked the small places, the concrete cracks and hidden nooks. They were good for hiding in, and that's very important. When you've got Dennis Hodgson and his meat-head friends after you, you need to disappear fast.

Tommy hadn't always been bullied. It seemed to happen when he hit eight. It was strange how up until that point he'd been pretty non-descript. Now it was like the world knew who he was and wanted to ridicule him. He didn't suppose he was the first boy to be picked on by Dennis. In fact, Dennis had a collection of poor souls that he enjoyed tormenting. But Tommy had had enough. He was tired of running. For the longest time he wished he could just become invisible, like in all the books he read. He imagined what it would be like every day. And if he squeezed his eyes shut, really closed them tight so that the dark of his eyelids sent blurry patterns to his mind, then maybe, just maybe it might happen.

And perhaps that's how it did happen; because he willed too hard. Because he was out of breath from running and tired, and he couldn't stand the stampede of Dennis's feet? One minute he was crouched behind the prickly yellow rose bush at the back of the school gates, and the next he was some place completely different. No sign of Dennis or his cronies, no sign of anything familiar.

'Oh my!' he said, rubbing his eyes through a hem of fringe.

But the picture was the same. He was sitting in the middle of a dense wood; except it was bigger than any wood he'd seen before. It was more like a forest. The trees were a mixture, from the tall and slender, with silvery bark, to the fatter twisted ones that spread their branches in every direction. When he looked up, he could hardly make out the sky. The web of leaves let only slithers of light through.

Tommy shivered. He wasn't sure about this at all. Yes, he'd wanted to disappear, but this place seemed awful creepy to him.

'Where am I?' he asked, and to his surprise a tiny voice answered.

'You're in the First Forest.'

He looked around but could only see a small blue and gold dragonfly.

'Did you say that?' he asked.

'Yes, of course I did!' the dragonfly snapped.

'Oh' Tommy shrugged. 'Where I come from, dragonflies don't speak.'

'Well that's silly,' the dragonfly chuckled. 'So what brings you here?'

'I don't know. I'm sort of lost.' And Tommy began to stretch his legs. 'I wanted to be invisible, but I ended up here, and I need to find my way back.'

The dragonfly buzzed around his head. 'Can't help you there.' it sang, and then shot up into the branches of a nearby tree.

Tommy called after it, but the dragonfly had already gone. This really was a mess. He was stuck in some other world where insects spoke, and the trees seemed to creep up on you. He looked around him. Yes, the trees really did seem to have moved closer! He made a run for it, but a bumbling oak thudded a heavy branch in his path. He turned around, and one of the silvery birches was right behind him, it's trunk swaying.

'And what have we here?' came a thundering voice. It had to be the oak.

'Looks like a man child,' a female voice joined in.

'Well we didn't invite him, and that's not good.'

'I'll say it's not good! I propose we crush him till he squeaks,' came a third, gravelly voice.

'No!' Tommy screamed. 'No please don't.'

'They won't do anything!'

It was a girl's voice, and Tommy looked up to see an elfin-looking creature nestling high in the branches of a birch tree. He had never seen a girl like her. She had hair that sprouted from her head like a huge bush of fire. And her eyes were the greenest green, like the emerald stone earrings his mother wore.

'Don't listen to the trees. They're old and wary of strangers. They won't hurt you.'

Tommy fumbled nervously from foot to foot. 'Who are you?'

'I'm Tat Rootwhistle, daughter of the forest, playmate of the stars.' She jumped to the ground landing without the slightest sound.

'Who are you?' she asked.

'I'm Tommy.'

'So what brings you to the First Forest, Tommy?'

'I don't know.' he muttered. 'I'm lost. One minute I was hiding in the school playground, the next I was here.'

'Hiding?' And Tat grinned. 'Oh I love hiding, it's my favourite game.'

And with that she was gone. Tommy didn't even blink. He spun around with his arms, he ran from tree to tree, but there was simply no sign of her.

'I'm here!' she laughed, and stepped from out of nowhere.

'How did you do that?'

'It's a gift I have. I turn sideways, stay very still, and people mistake me for a bush, or a clump of grass. They see what they expect to see. It's something I've learned over time. I could teach you, if you'd like?'

Tommy sighed. 'Yes, I'd like. But first I need to find my way home.'

Tat took his hand. Her skin felt hot and dry, like the flames of a bonfire.

'We'll find a way back for you. Don't worry.'

They began to walk, out of the glade of trees and deeper along the shadowy paths.

Back at the school gates Dennis Hodgson had come a cropper. He'd steamed towards the rose bush with the full intention of flattening that weed Tommy, only to find that he'd disappeared! Instead Dennis had fallen head over feet into the bush, thorns sticking into hands and legs and, most uncomfortable of all, his big fleshy bottom. It wasn't a pretty sight, as Dennis tried to clamber to his feet. The pain from a thousand angry thorns made his eyes water.

'Tommy!' He yelled. 'I'll find you, you snivelling worm. I'll make you pay.'

But really, he was puzzled. How could Tommy vanish like that? It didn't make any sense. He felt defeated, cheated out of his afternoon sport. He leaned over the bush, nursing his sore bottom with his free hand. There was no hole there; no way Tommy could have escaped through the fence. He scratched his head, and thought long and hard. Something that Dennis Hodgson very rarely did because thoughts hurt, at least, some of his did. Truth be told, he wasn't very happy inside. He didn't like himself, and he didn't think anyone else would unless he made them.

He didn't know why he hated Tommy so much. It wasn't that he'd done anything to upset Dennis. In fact the boy was as quiet as a mouse most of the time. But there was something that made him feel good every time he made the boy squirm. It meant the other kids laughed at him, they liked being with him. So he just did it more and more. Picking on Tommy was easy and he supposed that had something to do with it. It made him feel important. It meant he got noticed, which had always been hard for Dennis. At home he had to compete with three brothers, but here in the playground everybody knew who he was. He smiled; the small quiet kids were always the best. If only I could find you Tommy, Dennis thought, closing his eyes and gritting his teeth. If only, then I'd make you pay, then everything would feel all right again.

When he opened his eyes again, the school had disappeared. The concrete beneath his feet was now a soft slope of mud; eyeballs blinked from every corner, small animal twitching eyes, peering from murky branches.

'Whoa, this is weird,' said Dennis, and he pulled his jacket tighter to him.

'Tommy, are you out there?' His voice was a grunt, and it bounced off the trees making him jump. 'If this is a trick, you know I'll get you!'

Still nothing.

'Tommy?' he tried again. 'If you're out there, you better let me know, or I'll swear I'll batter you!' But the only reply was his echo dancing on the breeze.

Then behind a rustle of leaves, a hideous groaning sound that made Dennis catch his breath.

'What makes you think he'll answer?' came the voice, low and threatening.

Slowly Dennis turned, his face twisted with fright.

'What makes you think he'd want to talk to you?'

It was a spider, but not the kind of spider you would normally see. It was a giant furry thing about the size of a kitten, with long bobbly legs and huge yellow globes of eye.

Dennis screamed and began to run, but his foot snagged on a weed and he fell to the ground, grazing his knee.

'Don't hurt me, please don't hurt me,' he whimpered.

'Why should I want to hurt you, little boy? I have better things to do with my time.'

The spider moved close. Its eyes were bright like diamonds.

'I wouldn't try looking for your friend. He doesn't want to be found. That's why he came here in the first place. But then, you'd know all about that. You were the one that made him feel that way.'

Dennis shivered. He did know all about that. Right now he wished he were a thousand miles away. The spider seemed to smile; it's broken glass teeth leered.

'It's not very nice to be scared is it?'

'I didn't mean to scare him, not really.'

'But you did. Didn't you realise how you made him feel?'

Dennis sniffed. 'I didn't think about it.'

'Well maybe you should have done. It's not too late now, you can always change things,' the spider snapped.

Then it sprang in the air and Dennis let out a sob of relief. Change things, he thought. If he could change things he'd be a different person, one that didn't have to force people to like him.

Tommy and Tat had heard the screams.

'The wind has a way of carrying messages in this place,' Tat had told him.

'I wonder what that was?' Tommy shook his head. 'It didn't sound good.'

'Maybe, maybe not. This is an old forest. It has to protect itself from harm. It can usually tell a person's heart. It deals with them depending on their true nature.'

'What's that mean?' Tommy was starting to get annoyed by her way of talking in riddles. They'd walked for what seemed like forever, but every place looked the same to him; dark, dreamy, just not quite real.

'It means that if you're good, then good will find you. Like me, I was sent to help you out. But if you're bad, then you're only going to draw the bad things. It's nature.'

'So do you live here?' Tommy asked.

'Yes, sort of. Although I'd really like to live everywhere.'

'You wouldn't like to live in my world.'

'But that's only because you're unhappy,' said Tat. 'If that wasn't the case, you'd see things differently.'

'If only there was no more Dennis Hodgson,' Tommy said.

'There would always be something to make you sad. You have to turn it around, Tommy, that's the only way. And anyway, if you're that unhappy why do you want to go back? You could stay here with me.' She motioned to the sky, with her brittle, twig-like arms. 'We could have so much fun. I could show you how to fly through the trees, and chase a rainbow to its end. There are all sorts of things I could teach you.'

'I'm sorry, Tat. I have to go home. That's where I belong. I just don't want to at the moment.'

She shrugged her bony shoulders, 'Okay, I guess. But that doesn't mean we can't have some fun before you go!'

Without saying a word she dragged Tommy down a rough pebbled slope, down until they reached a small brook of inky water. Their feet skidded on the path, and it felt to Tommy like they were flying.

'This is fun!' he yelled.

'See, I told you so!' called Tat. 'Whoopee!'

'Whoopee to you too!'

But then a sound broke through their hoots of laughter.

'Tat Rootwhistle, is that you causing all that racket?'

Tommy realised it was the old brook talking, its waters bubbling with each word.

'It sure is!'

'Well come a little closer, girl, so I can see you! Oh and bring that friend of yours too. My eyesight's not as good as it used to be.'

Tommy and Tat exchanged glances. He was getting to like the strangeness of this place. It was full of magical surprises. They moved to the water's edge and crouched together.

'What brings you to my waters, lad?' the brook hissed.

'He's lost,' Tat answered. 'He wants to find his way back home.'

'I see. And how did you end up here in the first place? Were you running from something?'

Tommy gasped. 'How did you know?'

'I know most things, and people like you end up here for one reason. They are looking to escape their world. You must have wanted to get away pretty badly? And I'm guessing there is only one way back for you.'

'What's that?' asked Tat, letting her fingers tickle the edge of the water.

'Well it's obvious. He's going to have to want to be there, to want to be a part of his old life again. Until he does, he'll have to stay here.'

'Oh,' Tat sighed. 'That's not so good.'

She looked at Tommy and smiled sweetly. 'Whatever you're scared of is preventing you from going back. You have to turn it around, Tommy, you have to.'

'But there's something you should know too,' the brook chattered on, 'something that could help.'

Its black surface rippled and cleared until a series of pictures formed.

'That's Dennis!' pointed Tommy. 'It looks like he's here in the wood.'

'The forest,' Tat corrected.

'But what's he doing here?'

He watched as the image of his bully curled and retreated, and cried like a baby from the brook's mouth. Then the brook spoke again, and this time his voice was softer.

'He's here for the same reason as you, me lad. He's trying to escape. Somehow he ended up following you. But he doesn't look too happy about it now.'

'But Dennis isn't scared of anything.'

'Everyone's scared of something,' said Tat. 'Come on, we have to find him and help him.'

'Why should I?' asked Tommy.

'Because he needs help, and because deep down you know it's the right thing to do. Just because he's been bad to you, doesn't mean he's all bad. You don't know how other people treat him.'

Tommy sighed, 'They usually do everything he says.'

'Ah but that's only what you see Tommy, and you don't see everything. You know, everyone deserves a second chance, even Dennis.' She held out her hand. 'Come on, let's find him and then maybe you'll be able to go home.'

'Thanks, Mr Brook,' she called – as they scrambled up the hill.

Dennis had never been fond of trees. His only involvement with them had been when he was etching his name or something rude in their bark with his penknife. It was something fun to do at the park, when he wasn't stealing pocket money off the younger kids. So when the trees began to bend inwards Dennis started to panic. It wasn't just a gust of wind that brought the branches daringly close; it was something else. When, after a couple of minutes, they began prodding him, and wrapping vines around his ankles, he began to shout. He wriggled and kicked, but his legs were caught tight. There was nothing he could do. The more he struggled the more the gummy vines dug into his skin.

'Look at him! Little foolish worm!'

'Fat little foolish worm!'

The trees chanted.

'Trying to break free, but he can't because he's stupid.'

'What's the matter, don't you like playing with us? You're normally not so shy!'

'Perhaps we should carve our names into your flesh? Isn't that what you like to do?'

'No, please. I'm sorry. I'm really sorry.'

'It's a bit late for that don't you think?' The voices shouted together.

'And what's to say you won't do it again?'

'I won't, I won't,' Dennis snivelled. 'Honestly I won't.'

'We don't believe you,' they bellowed, and sent him rocking this way and that. Tossing him from side to side like a stone.

'You're in the First Forest now. The kingdom of the trees; it's where it all began. Once little worm, all the trees were like us. They could move and talk. It's only time and mankind that have changed them. It's your sort that have made them weak, did you know that?'

Dennis began to cry. 'I'm sorry. I'm really sorry. If I could change I would.'

'Change!' they yelled. 'Do you really think you can change, little worm?'

'Yes,' sobbed Dennis. 'I'd like to.'

'And what about everything else you've done? You've been bad, you're rotten to the core!'

'I know, but I didn't mean it,' he yelped. 'I just wanted people to like me; I wanted them to notice me.'

'But don't you see, little worm, they don't like you at all. They're scared of you. They may laugh at your jokes, or the bullying you get up to, but it's only because they're afraid. How can you call them real friends?'

'I don't know,' sighed Dennis. 'I'd not thought of it like that before.'

'Maybe not, but it's too late now. What's done is done.'

Just at that moment the air was split in two as Tat and Tommy came sailing through the foliage. Tat was gripping a rope, which she used to glide through the trees, and Tommy had his hands wrapped around her waist.

'Tommy?' Dennis spluttered. 'Tommy, is that you?'

Tommy smiled. 'Yes it is, and this is my friend Tat. Tat Rootwhistle.'

'You don't look too happy down there,' she added.

Dennis blinked back a tear.

'Tommy, I'm sorry, I'm so sorry. Please help me; please get these things off me.'

Tat looked down on him, her hair even wilder than usual.

'Shall we help him, Tommy? After all, he's the reason you are here in the first place?'

He looked at Tat and shrugged.

'I don't know, Tat.'

'I know I don't deserve your help,' said Dennis. 'Not after everything I've done, but I'm going to try and be different. I'm not proud of any of it. Truth is I've never really liked myself that much.'

'Well, that makes two of us,' grinned Tommy, 'but as a good friend of mine once told me, everyone deserves a second chance.'

When Tommy and Dennis jumped back into the real world nothing had changed; school was the same, lunchtime break was nearly over and the time had barely moved, but something between them had grown. Dennis was quiet. He forced a smile, and shuffled about uncomfortably. Tommy took that as a sign that he was still feeling bad for everything and didn't know what to say. He on the other hand was bright and cheery. Things were different now he knew about this other world. He felt like he'd been let into a secret, a special secret. It was something that only he and Dennis could talk about, although he could tell Dennis wasn't too keen on remembering what had happened, but maybe that would change. After all, Dennis was trying to turn over a new leaf. They had slipped back as quickly as they had vanished. It had all been a matter of will, of wanting to return without fear or hatred. He'd just had enough time to say his goodbyes to the trees after they'd released Dennis from their grip, and to Tat. She had given him a sprig of hawthorn as a parting gift, from the curls of her hair.

'It will keep you safe,' she'd said. 'And it will help you to remember me and this place.'

'Oh I won't forget,' Tommy had replied. 'How could I ever forget the First Forest and meeting you? It's been brilliant.'

She had smiled sadly and shook her head.

'You will, it's just a matter of time.

'Will you forget me?' he asked shyly.

But the swirl of memory, and wishing spells, had chosen that moment to take them and return them to the rose bush in the playground. He never heard her answer.

Tat dangled her feet in the cool waters of the brook. 'Do you think he'll ever come back?' she asked the sparkling depths.

The brook bubbled and chuntered and finally answered. 'If he does, then it will be because he's lost again. And that's not so good.'

'I suppose so,' sighed Tat. 'I suppose I shouldn't wish for it but I keep hoping that perhaps he won't forget, like all the others before him.'

The brook flickered softly. 'It's called growing up, Tat.' Then it swirled into a glistening circle. 'Here, take a look at this.'

And so she did, peering closer to the mirror image. She saw Tommy standing by the yellow rose bush, twiddling the sprig of hawthorn between his fingers with a thoughtful look in his eye.

'He remembers me!' she grinned. 'He really does remember me.'

'For now, it seems so,' the brook replied.

But it was too late, she was already gone, singing and giggling along the grassy banks. Just a wild girl, with fiery hair, in a place beyond time and space.

The Butterfly Boy –
a Tat Rootwhistle tale

The following story was inspired by a documentary about a boy named Jonny Kennedy, entitled 'The Boy Whose Skin Fell Off'. Jonny suffered with an incurable skin disease called epidermolysis bullosa (EB for short). EB is a terrible condition whereby the skin separates and blisters at the slightest touch. It means that children with EB are denied a normal life of play and cuddles. They are covered in bandages, which they have to have changed regularly, causing immense pain. They have blisters that need to be lanced and this means several injections a day to fight infection. In some severe cases the blisters line the stomach and so sufferers have to be fed through a drip. Most children with EB live till their early thirties, but by this stage the skin on their hands and feet has fused and they are wheelchair bound.

Because EB affects the skin it means that sufferers look different and this can often cause alarm to other children who do not understand about the condition. When I wrote 'The Butterfly Boy' I wanted to educate and inform children about this disease, and also to motivate children to look for the best in a situation. Everyone is special, and there is always something fantastic that they can give to the world. In Jonny's case he has inspired and touched millions of people around the world.

Sometimes it feels like I'm sitting at this window forever. Not that I mind. I like the window; I like its shape, and the way it opens up the world. The garden is only a footstep away. I can see the roses that Dad planted and the lawn with its smooth slope down to the rockery. The pond where Jimmy sits poking the frogs – he likes tormenting them. Eliza is playing with a ball. She's aiming it at the wall, and every so often Dad pulls a face. She must have fired it close to the bathroom window. I watch them all and I smile. My family, they're great.

Then, of course, there's me – Billy Shaw (I joke that it should actually be Billy Sore, but my mum says that's not funny). Life's not so simple with me around. I can't do much. Well actually that's a lie. I can do plenty in my head, it's just

I'm not that mobile. I'm also in pain a lot of the time. You see I have this skin thing; I was born with it. They call it EB for short, which is just as well because I can't pronounce it's real name. My tongue just won't fit around the words. Anyway, it means my skin blisters at the slightest touch. Mum has to change my dressings every day because of infection. It's hurts a lot, and sometimes I scream out. I know she doesn't mean to hurt me; it's just something that has to be done. A part of the morning routine. Everything has a routine in our house, but I guess that's just because things need to happen. Life goes on. So you could say my staring out of the window on a Sunday afternoon is just a part of that same string of events that is my life. I could go outside I suppose, but the sun hurts my eyes. And anyway, if I did, I'd miss Tat's visits.

Tat. She's a strange one. I can't remember when she first showed up. I've known her for so long that I just expect to see her now. She's not what you'd call normal, with her wild thatch of red hair. All sorts of creatures live in her hair, but she doesn't seem to mind. She's small and wiry and she springs through the trees almost as fast as the wind. She looks a bit ragged and scruffy, but that's what you'd expect from a wild girl. She comes from the First Forest, a place beyond our world. She says it's a magical place, a giant wood filled with enchantment. I'd like to go there some day, and she says I could, but I'm not so sure I'd be able to. She says if I think really hard I could almost be there, that it's that easy. You just step over from one world to another. I wish it was! I almost feel like I know it though. I can picture it so well in my head. The tall spindly trees like giants' legs, the emerald green of the forest floor, and the flowers. Tat says there are flowers of every colour, beautiful purple daisies, silver and gold buttercups and even spotted roses. Can you imagine that?

Of course, I haven't told anyone else about Tat's visits. They wouldn't believe me. I know they'd think I'd made her up to amuse myself, to wile away the hours. But it's not true. She's as real as you or me, it's just she comes from some place else. Except that today she doesn't come at all. There's no sweet smell of honey, or the faint breeze that she brings with her from the First Forest. And although I know she has a life outside of here, it's weird that she hasn't showed up. She always appears at the same time on a Sunday, five minutes after three, time for afternoon tea. She likes my mum's homemade scones. She likes most things.

Now I'm not one for panicking, or worrying. Having EB makes you appreciate the little things in life, and well, I just like to get on with things. But I must admit I'm starting to think something is wrong. Tat just wouldn't disappear on me like that. We're pretty good friends, she'd tell me if she were going away. I know she would! Thing is, I don't know how to contact her, other than thinking about her really hard. That usually does the trick. But if something is wrong, then she wouldn't be able to hear me, so there's no point. I close my eyes. If only there was a way to reach the First Forest. I've pictured it so many times. A large open glade, filled with sunlight. A cluster of trees, and eyes peering from corners, from cracks and holes in the wood. What sorts of magical creatures would live there? I have my theories. I can imagine all sorts of curious looking birds, with great fan-like wings and musical voices. They'd have strange names too, like Mucklebeak and Thornyfoot. Then again, Tat's Tat Rootwhistle and you can't find a much stranger name than that. I bet the Forest would smell nice too. Not your usual woody outdoors smells, no this would be different. It would be herby almost but sweet, like mint, the kind of smell you long to pop into your mouth and taste. The wind would be gentle, like a fairy tickling your nose. You'd feel it tap-dancing upon your head, making a mess of your hair. Yes, it would send a shiver up your spine. I can feel it now. I can feel the slow crawl of excitement as it moves up my back; the breeze gives my cheek a dry kiss. It's comforting. I open my eyes, and bingo. I'm here! I'm really here, in the First Forest. Sitting on a pile of twigs. But the pile of twigs is moving, shifting under my legs. It's weird, I can't feel it as such; it's like being here, but not really being here. It's like my mind has escaped my body and brought me to this place.

'Would you please get off me!'

I rise, floating upwards. I'm not in control of my body, or this new shape. It's going to take a while to get used to moving around. But I'm not moving in the normal sense of the word; I'm almost flying!

'I'm sorry,' I say. Warmth fills my throat. At least my voice sounds the same.

'That's what they all say. But it's too late by then, I'm already half way to being flattened.'

'What are you?'

I look at the strange collection of sticks, and at the conker, which appears to be a head.

'What do I look like?' the little voice replies.

'Some sort of stick man?'

'Hooray, give the boy a medal. He's got it right. I'm a man, made of sticks. It's not that difficult is it?'

'I'm sorry,' I say again.

'The problem with your sort is that you don't really look at anything. You see a pile of sticks and so you stamp on them. Like the way they sound when they snap do you? You wouldn't like it if it were your arm or leg!'

'I'm sorry.'

'Stop apologising,' he snaps. 'And anyway, who are you and what are you doing here?'

'I'm Billy, Billy Shaw, and I'm looking for my friend Tat Rootwhistle.'

The stick man cocks his head on one side.

'Tat Rootwhistle, eh?'

'You know her?'

'Of course I know her, everyone knows who Tat is!'

I'm about to say sorry again, but I stop myself. My body is bobbing up and down in the air like a balloon.

'Am I really here, in the First Forest?'

'What do you think?' the stick man sighs. 'There are trees, and flowers, look around you.'

'Yes, I know that. It's just, well I'm not quite myself.'

'You're in spirit form. That's how you're able to visit here.

'So I've left my body back home?'

'In a way,' he grins. 'You don't look too happy up there.'

'I'm not!'

'Well just think yourself to the ground. That's all you have to do. Imagine you're standing still and it will happen. Goodness do you people have to be told everything?'

I have to say it sounds easy enough, and to be honest, it is. Once I get the hang of the fact that everything I do is a thought in my head I can move almost normally.

'So do you know where I'll find Tat?' I ask.

The stick man shakes his head. 'I don't, but I know someone who might be able to help you.' He starts off in the direction of the trees.

'Hey, wait a minute,' I say, remembering to send a message to my legs to scramble after him.

We've been walking for quite a while now. The stick man is only small, about the size of a rabbit, but he can move fast. His strides are jerky, and he rocks from to side to side. I find that I can keep up if I tell myself to glide. It's almost like being a ghost, not that I'd know what being a ghost is like. But I imagine that's how I must look.

The stick man mutters away to himself. 'I've told her before about wandering off, about sticking her nose into other people's business.'

'You think she's in trouble?'

'Oh Tat, you silly, silly girl,' he tuts, completely ignoring my question.   'I wish you'd listen to me.'

I fall behind, and leave him to his grumbling. He's not the friendliest sort, but I reckon he has his reasons. Can't be much fun if people keep trying to step on you. I suppose it must be difficult when nobody notices you're there. In my case it's the other way round. Everyone notices me; they can't help it because I look different. Sometimes that's hard, but I'm getting used to people staring. They call us butterfly children, children with EB. I like that. It sounds nice and today I'm feeling pretty much like a butterfly, floating around, twisting and turning and dancing between leaves. It's a good feeling.

'We're here!' the stick man yells. He's slipping down a mossy bank, heading for the stream.

'Where are we?'

'At the babbling brook.'

'Oh.'

'Well are you coming or not?'

I nod. What more can I say?

The brook, as you might have guessed, is magical. It's talks, well it babbles to be more precise. It, which is a he, is very friendly. His voice reminds me of my grandad's, all soft and wrinkly around the edges. He doesn't seem surprised at Tat's disappearance. Instead he sighs, and I watch as his waters spiral and ripple into a picture. It's as clear as looking into a mirror.

'You're right, look, she's in trouble and she needs your help.'

The stick man grumbles, and the brook tells him to be quiet.

I peer into the waters, careful not to get too close to the reflection, which keeps breaking apart.

'Where is she?' I ask.

I can see she's trapped, her leg caught on something. Her face is very pale, the usual fiery glint gone from her eyes. She's leaning against a tree, and there are dirty tearstains on her cheeks.

'She'll be over the other side of the river, probably to the West near the Soulless Plains,' says the stick man. 'I told her to be careful, not to wander too far.'

'Nagging will do no good,' says the brook. 'You have to rescue her. There's nothing I can do from here. I'm helpless.'

'Well what can I do?' whines the stick man.

I was going to ask the same thing, but hold my tongue; after all, I'm not made of sticks.

'You can show the lad here how to find her.'

'And when I do, what if I can't help?' I ask.

The brook's waters bubble and then return to silvery stillness.

'There is always something you can do. You should know that.'

We set off on our journey, travelling through the heart of the First Forest, the stick man's stiff little actions leading the way. I try talking to him, and after a while he seems to cheer up. I suppose it takes time to trust people. I wonder what my mum and dad are doing right now. Will they be wondering where I am? I must have been gone for a couple of hours. Oh dear. They'll be worrying. Mum will probably be doing her nut. She's bad enough anyway, but with me having EB, well it just makes her that bit more protective. Its strange this flying business. I'm not tired at all. I suppose if anything my head feels tight from all this thinking – thinking about keeping off the ground, thinking about gliding in the right direction, thinking about not crashing into that tree. But I'm doing okay. I'm rather pleased with myself. I wish Tat was here because she'd be pleased too. I think she gets quite angry with me because I often don't feel like doing anything. I tell her she doesn't understand what it's like, and she just wags a finger at me and says 'stop being such a baby'. She's only trying to make me feel better.

'That's my job done!' the stick man says, stamping both twig-legs into the ground.

'Is this it?'

'Sure looks like it.' He points down the slope.

I follow his gaze and that's when I see her, still slumped against the tree trunk.

'Tat, Tat!' I yell.

I swoop down towards her, enjoying the fast rush of air against my cheek.

'Billy?' She looks up; her eyes are huge and red-rimmed. 'Billy is that really you? What are you doing here?'

'I came to find you silly.'

She tries to smile. 'I'm a bit stuck.'

'I can see that.'

'It's my leg. I was about to climb this tree, but I slipped, the bark was a bit damp and well the next thing I know my leg's stuck down some kind of hole. But it feels like something's cutting into my ankle. I was afraid. I thought I'd be stuck here for days.'

'Have you tried moving it?'

'I've tried everything.' She sighs, 'It's useless.'

'Let me see.' I push my head close to the ground, it's almost as if the soil is gripping on to her foot. From what I've seen so far, nothing would surprise me with this place.

'It looks like the earth is clutching your leg.'

'It feels like it's trying to pull me under.' Her eyes well up. 'I was only going to do a bit of tree-hopping.'

Tree-hopping is Tat's favourite pastime. She springs from branch to branch like a trapeze artist. I've seen her do it in my garden and, boy, is she good!

'Don't worry. I'll get you out of here, I promise.'

'But it hurts, it really hurts.'

I smile. 'I know. But you know what you'd say to me don't you?'

'Stop being such a baby,' she smiles. 'Yes I would.'

'Wait there a minute,' I say. 'I think I've got the answer.'

I soar back up the hill, my nose almost flat to the ground. I'm looking for something that I know will help. It's not too long before I spot it.

'Stick man!'

'Oh not you again.' He shakes his head. 'I thought I was rid of you.'

'But you can help, you can save the day.'

'And what if I don't want to? Can't a poor old group of sticks be left in peace for just one moment? I've done my bit, I brought you here, and anyway what can I do. I'm made of sticks remember?'

'There's always something you can do,' I say, remembering the brook's words to me.

'That's easy for you to say.'

'Don't you want to be a hero?' I whisper.

'I want to be lots of things, but it never happens.'

I tell him the plan and he sighs and whinges in all the right places. Deep down I think he's delighted to be asked, but he'd never let on. We go back to Tat, who has a terrible giggling fit when she sees him. It doesn't go down too well, but he's a generous sort despite appearances. He wriggles down into the soil, brushing her leg, until I can only make out the tip of his conker head. Then after much 'hrumphing' he turns on his side, his arms out-stretched, pushing the soil further apart. I can see the gap; it's only there for a second so I have to move fast. I grab Tat's leg and pull. She falls back against the tree. There's a squeal and the muffled sound of shouting.

'We did it!' I say.

'Yes we did,' grins Tat. 'Thank you both so much.'

'But what about …?'

I look at the patch of soil where her foot was stuck.

'Where's he gone?'

Her mouth drops, 'He'll be stuck inside, just like I was. The soil will have dragged him down.'

'But we can't leave him there. We've got to try and get him out.'

I begin clawing at the ground, but it's solid like a brick.

'I don't understand. One minute there was a hole, now nothing.'

'This place is alive Billy.' She kneels next to me, her tiny fingers stabbing at the earth. 'I don't think this is going to work,' she says.

There's a thundering sound from above, a sound like the sky is about to crack open. It reminds me of the aeroplanes that fly over our house back home, and so I look up but there's nothing there.

'Leave the stick man,' a gruff voice says. It comes from behind, shaking the fat bark of the tree trunk.

'Is that the tree talking?' I whisper.

Tat shrugs, her eyes look like they're about to pop out of her head.

'I said leave the stick man. He's safe, he's with me, deep beneath the earth in my roots. He'll be fine, he'll be born again as part of me, part of this tree.'

'Is he really all right?' I ask Tat.

'Well he did come from a tree in the first place. So I suppose he can't be in any real danger.'

I nod, not that I'm convinced, but what can I do?

'I say we leave. The trees are the oldest, most respected beings in the forest. They wouldn't hurt anyone.' She smiles. 'Honestly. I'm sure he'll be fine.'

She takes my hand and we're off, and I have to say I'm glad. That talking tree was starting to give me the creeps.

Tat recovers fast. She's so full of beans sailing through the trees, springing from branch to branch as if her knees were made of rubber bands. I follow, gliding this way and that, curving and twirling to avoid branches; skimming the forest floor, and diving towards the stream that moves like a snake below us. It's so exciting. I really am a butterfly, beautiful and fragile. I'm a soaring, spinning boy dancing through the heart of the forest. Nothing can stop me. Nothing can hurt me, and that's a feeling I want to hold on to.

'You should be going home soon,' Tat says.

'Home.' I let the word tickle my lips. I hadn't thought about it. I'd lost myself for a while there in the forest, but I know that I can't escape forever.

'You can always come back,' she grins. 'Whenever you want to. You've proved how easy it is today.'

'I know,' I smile.

I'll be honest, I'm not sure if I want to go back home. Part of me likes this new shape, likes being without pain for a while. But then I'd miss my family, and there are so many other things that I enjoy.

'I'll come and visit you, soon,' Tat says.

'You only come for my mum's scones,' I laugh.

'Mmmmmm, scones!' She licks her lips. 'Well they are very nice!'

We say our goodbyes quickly. Tat does that thing where she wrinkles her nose and waves. I'm not sure what I expect, or how hard I think going back will be, but it all happens fast. One minute I close my eyes, then I open them to find another pair of eyes hovering above me. Perfume fills my nose, and it starts to twitch.

'Mum?'

'Oh Billy, you're awake. I was getting so worried.'

And then to my dad, 'John, Billy's awake, he's okay.'

'Well of course he's okay.' My dad comes into view. His broad sun-tanned features relax into a smile. 'You had us going for a bit there son. We couldn't wake you! We wondered where you'd gone to.'

'You wouldn't believe me if I told you.'

He shakes his head. 'You and that over-active imagination.'

I look out of the window. The lawn is shaded now the sun has gone in. The roses are bowing their pink heads; up and down they jig on the gentle breeze. I think I see something out of the corner of my eye. Yes I do see something. Its quick and nimble, and it's heading for the bush at the end of the garden. It can't be, but it is. I don't believe it! There's a little stick man on the grass. We have a stick man in our garden!

I start to laugh.

'What is it Billy?' Mum's got that look of worry in her eyes. 'Just a private joke,' I say, although I can't wait to tell Tat. She'll think it's a hoot. But then life is, sometimes.

This window is my favourite spot. It opens up into my garden, and into other worlds too; worlds that I can return to any time I want – with a little imagination.

Playing by Numbers – a tale of data handling*

Sophie hated hockey. She hated the fact that she could never run fast enough to get to the ball, and that other people's hockey sticks seemed always to end up clattering around her ankles. It was hardly a surprise that no one ever picked her for their team. Most of all though Sophie hated the arguments. There was always some dispute or other centred around the game and Emily Hunt was usually at the heart of it. This time she'd started before they'd even got on the pitch. They were in the changing rooms and Emily was holding court. Her thin lips stretched to a sparkling smile, her blonde curls tied loosely in a bow.

'You know I'm the best,' she was saying to her groupies. 'It's been proved, and anyway that's why Miss Johnson made me team captain.'

'Well I can tackle better than anybody,' Lucy Watkins added.

Emily shook her head and a curl escaped in her eye.

'You can't tackle better than me and you know it.'

'Yes I can!'

Sophie turned from the window. 'Why don't you all shut up!' she snapped.

She didn't know where it had come from, but the words fell from her mouth and landed with a loud slap on the floor. A locker door slammed, and six pairs of eyes regarded her with amusement.

'Ooooh er! Who do you think you are?'

'And who asked for your opinion loser?'

The insults started to fly thick and fast, as Sophie backed into the wall. She had to say something; she knew it. But what could she say, how could she stand up to them all? She'd always been the quiet one, the one nobody noticed at all.

'Are you saying you don't think I'm the best hockey player in the school, Sophie Elliot?'

It was Emily, her grin ever expanding.

'No, I never said that,' Sophie sighed. 'But where's your proof?' She took a breath. 'I mean how can you say that you're the best when you don't have any evidence?'

She wasn't sure why she said it, but something clicked in her head.

It was as if a tiny voice had taken over her thoughts.

'What do you mean evidence? It's obvious I'm the best. I wouldn't be picked for the top team if I weren't.'

'That still doesn't mean anything, you have to look at the larger picture. You have to do a proper survey.'

Emily wrinkled her nose and the other girls sniggered.

'What the hell does she mean, survey? Ignore her!'

But Emily wasn't about to walk away with her pride in question.

'Okay then. We will do a survey. We'll ask everyone in the school, and then we'll see. Meet me here this time tomorrow, and you'd better pray that I'm right otherwise …'

And she crunched her fist and raised it in front of Sophie's nose.

Why did I do that, Sophie thought, and really, where did the silly idea of a survey come from?

'From me!' came the voice inside her head. Or was it inside her head, because it sounded close to her left ear.

Sophie swung round, one way and then the other. There was no one there.

'Great, now I'm hearing things!' she grumbled.

'Me too! Isn't it fun?'

Sophie turned around again, and that's when she saw him; a funny little eyeball of a man with tiny stick arms and legs. He was a strange shade of purple, a bit like her mother's amethyst necklace, and he looked ridiculous with one huge iris, blinking.

'Name's Data Cruncher, Master Data Cruncher to be correct.'

He held out a wiry arm. Sophie edged closer, there was no one else around, the changing room was deserted as the other kids were out on the field. Everything seemed to have frozen in time.

'Are you real?' she asked.

'Are you?' he replied with a smile.

'I don't know what to say.'

'I know.' He grinned again. 'I heard you earlier. You were a bit lost for words, that's why I helped out.'

'You helped out? You were the one who got me to say those things?'

'Yes, clever of me wasn't it?'

'Not really,' Sophie sighed. 'Now I'm in even more of a mess. It's bad enough that the other girls don't like me, but at least they never really noticed me. Now they think I'm ridiculous and Emily Hunt is out to get me for sure.'

The eyeball man blinked solemnly then leapt onto a ledge and perched with his arms and legs crossed.

'All you need is to play around with some data.'

'Data?'

'Yes, numbers, information ...'

'Numbers? What's that got to do with anything?'

'Numbers have everything to do with everything, that's the point.'

'But I'm useless at maths!'

'Ah but there are different ways of looking at figures. You call it Statistics, I call it Data Crunching.'

'Yeah, right.' Sophie shook her head.

The man sprang from his sitting position down to her side in a delicate pirouette.

'So this Emily girl is going to ask around, she's going to get all her friends to say she's the best at hockey, but that's doesn't prove anything. She's got to consider all sorts of factors.'

'Like what?'

'Like how long she's played it for starters, and how many times she's practised. You need to ask a representative sample.'

Sophie shrugged, 'I still don't understand.'

'Well how can she call herself the best unless she's got something to compare it to? She'd have to survey all the other hockey players in the school, and she'd have to look at how long they'd played it and how much they practised, and who they think is the best player, to come up with real data to support her argument. Then of course if she were really going to do it properly she'd have to do a tally chart and put all the information into a table. That's the only easy way to present these facts.'

'But I don't get how this will help me? If she doesn't come out top, I'm for it, that's what she said.'

The little man grinned; his mouth moved to reveal a row of perfectly filed and gleaming teeth.

'You leave that to me! There are other ways of impressing people besides bullying, and I've an idea.'

Afternoon break the following day came faster than Sophie expected. She'd been working hard, putting Data Cruncher's advice into practice and to be honest, she'd quite enjoyed herself. Maths could actually be fun, especially when you jiggled around with it. She'd got to talk to an entirely new set of girls; she'd got into creating charts and making them look good. In fact the day had flown by and now she was prepared. It was a good feeling to know that she'd done this. She'd conquered both her fear of maths and was now about to face the immovable Emily. Could she really do this? Her stomach fluttered with excitement.

'Okay squirt,' it was Emily's voice bouncing from the lockers, 'you really have asked for this.'

She pushed forward, a wall of several other girls behind her.

'My mates here say I'm the best at hockey, at netball, at whatever you want, and they've come to shut you up, for good!' She sniggered, 'How stupid are you? I'd at least have thought you'd have the sense to chicken out.'

Sophie chewed her lip. 'I'm not stupid! You're the one that's stupid. You think this proves anything? You see I've done a survey of hockey players in the school, past and present, and I've taken into consideration their views, the amount of games they've played, and won, and, well, I can honestly say that Jenny Simpson is the best hockey player this school has.'

She shoved her papers into Emily's face.

'What's this rubbish?'

'They're charts and stats I've done to support my theories.'

'Are you mad?' And Emily knocked them to the floor.

'No, but I am.'

The voice was deeper than the other girls' and seemed to waver above their heads. They looked up to see a sixth form girl with dyed red hair and black kohl-smudged eyes.

'I'm Jenny Simpson.'

Emily gulped. 'Oh, I didn't see you there.' The other girls turned to run.

'Seems like you weren't paying attention,' Jenny grinned. 'Perhaps you could help Sophie with her charts. She seems to have dropped them and that's a shame after all the hard work she's done.'

Emily nodded and began scrabbling on the floor.

Sophie smiled. 'Thank you Data Cruncher,' she whispered. And somewhere in another time and place, in a land where numbers grow larger than trees, a tiny eyeball of a man blinked his joy, and began to search for other ways to play around with data.

*This material has been provided by the RSS Centre for Statistical Education at Nottingham Trent University.

The Magic Box – a magical tale about self belief

Sam was a quiet boy. He didn't like fuss or noise. He just liked to get on with things, which was all well and good, until he moved schools. That's when everything changed. At his new school all of the children were loud. They would laugh at him and call him names and play silly jokes. Sam didn't like that. He just wanted to be left alone. To be able to do what he did best, and that was read. You see, Sam loved reading. He loved the way a book felt, the crispness of the pages, the smell of it. He loved to be able to escape into the pages and imagine he was one of the characters. It was another world, and Sam loved slipping into the magic of it. So when his parents moved house he became more engrossed in his books than ever before. He guessed that was why the other kids picked on him.

His only enjoyment of the week, apart from reading on his own, was a trip up the road to Mrs McKenzie's house. Mrs McKenzie was an old woman with a hump on her back and long grey hair which she kept wound tightly in a bun on the back of her head. Her eyesight was failing and she could barely make out words or letters any more, so Sam would go every Thursday night and read to her. He would read the local paper, then he would read from a book of her choice. He liked that. It meant he got to read different things so it was never boring. The other kids thought it was strange that Sam should do this. They thought Mrs McKenzie was a witch because she lived in a big old house with a creaky door, and had a black cat. Sam knew better. He knew there was something special about her, but in a nice way.

One Thursday Sam was doing his usual reading session. He'd had a particularly horrible day at school. The kids had been taunting him, calling him names in and out of class, so he wasn't feeling very bright. Mrs McKenzie looked him in the eye and said,

'Now then, lad, are you going to tell me what's bothering you today?'

Sam shrugged. 'It's like it everyday at school.' And he began to tell her just what it was like.

'I'd love to be more confident, to have some courage and face them, but I just feel so scared all the while,' He said finally.

Mrs McKenzie smiled. 'I see, well maybe I can help you with that.'

She pointed a crooked finger towards a tall dark cupboard against the wall. 'See that cupboard, lad, you just go over there and open the doors.'

So Sam did just that. He walked right up to the giant oak doors and pulled them open. There inside were shelves and shelves of boxes, small wooden boxes with strange patterns on each side and words engraved on each one. Words like 'Beauty', 'Success', 'Luck', 'Happiness', and the one that caught Sam's eye, 'Courage'.

'Now then, Sam, you just have a good look at those boxes and you pick the one that you want and bring it over here to the table,' she said.

Sam didn't hesitate. He knew exactly what he wanted and that was courage. He picked up the tiny box and placed it on the table between them.

'Is it magic?' he asked.

'In a way, yes it is,' she said. 'Now the deal is this. You can take this box away with you, and you can carry it with you in your pocket at all times, but you must never open it, because if you do, the magic won't work. And you must give it back when the time is right. So if you want some courage, you keep this box with you, and in a few days' time you'll feel much better.'

'Wow,' said Sam. 'Thank you, thank you so much!'

He went skipping home with the box firmly in his pocket.

That night, as Sam got ready for bed, he placed the box on his bedside table. It was strange, it didn't really look magic, and he was tempted to open the lid, but he remembered his promise to Mrs McKenzie. So instead he made a wish that everything would be better in the morning and he went to sleep.

The following day he carried the box everywhere. He kept it in his pocket and every time one of the other kids made a comment or laughed at him he gripped the box tight. He still felt scared, but he was able to hold his head up high, knowing that he had a piece of magic with him. As the days went on Sam grew less and less bothered by the bullying, he started to enjoy school again. He even started smiling more, which in turn made the other children want to talk to him. By the end of the week, Sam had made lots of friends and as the next week came he started to feel more and more confident. By Thursday he was really having fun, it was as if the fear had dropped from his shoulders like a cloak.

At his next reading session Mrs McKenzie asked him how school was and he told her.

'Oh it's so much better now. I don't feel scared any more, your magic box has really helped.'

'That's very good news, Sam.' She reached out her hand. 'So you can give me the box back now.'

Sam looked down nervously. He fingered the box in his pocket. It felt so good knowing it was there. How could he give it back? But then a promise was a promise and he knew better than to go back on his word.

'I guess so,' he said and he pulled the box slowly from his pocket. 'But there's just one thing. Can I look inside it now? Please!'

Mrs McKenzie sighed, 'I suppose so, after all the magic spell has done it's work. Go on then, open the lid.'

So gently Sam began to lift the latch and open the lid. His jaw dropped. His eyes were wide with surprise.

'I don't believe it! I don't understand,' he said. 'There's nothing in here, how can this be? Where's the magic that helped me?'

Mrs McKenzie smiled, 'Just because you can't see it, doesn't mean the magic's not there. Magic is everywhere, it's all around us, and because you believed in it, it worked for you.'

Sam shook his head. He didn't understand what she meant at all. How could there be magic if you couldn't see it? Even so he gave her back the box before he left that day.

The weeks that followed at school were happy ones, and Sam made lots of new friends who became old friends and he did very well in his schoolwork. As the years progressed and Sam got older he often wondered about the magic box and Mrs McKenzie. Perhaps she had been a witch after all? Even so, whenever Sam found himself in a situation where he felt uncomfortable or a little afraid, he would imagine that he still had that wooden box in his pocket and somehow, quite unbelievably, all the fear dropped away.

Only in Pictures – a Tat Rootwhistle tale

I have added some suggestions on how this tale could be used to create class activities that encourage listening, speaking and written work.

'I'm here!' cried Tat, as she stepped into the playground, but no one noticed the little wild girl with the thatch of raspberry hair. Just a movement of air, and nothing there, or so it would seem to those who didn't look closely. Only Emma glanced up from her sketchbook. She was drawing again. Letting her hand spin and turn, and transform the page into a spiral of colour. Emma noticed most things, even if she couldn't always describe them.

'Where did you come from?'

'The First Forest,' grinned Tat. 'Would you like to see?'

Emma smiled. 'Is it pretty?'

'Of course. You should see the trees, they go on forever.'

'That's not possible.'

'Anything's possible where I come from!'

And before Emma could reply, Tat had her by the hand.

Around and around the tumbling oak they went; skirts swishing, locks of billowing hair flying.

'Three times round, and three times old,
To the forest made of gold!'

Ask the class to repeat this phrase, or come up with a different rhyme that could take them to the First Forest. They might want to work on poems or chants and use them in their own Tat Rootwhistle story (see later suggestions).

In a shot they found themselves standing on a pile of leaves. Above, the trees twisted gold and amber in the sunshine.

'This is the First Forest?' asked Emma.

'Yes. Do you like it?'

'Oh my,' and her eyes stretched saucer-like. 'I wish I had my crayons with me. Look at the colours!'

You see, Emma didn't care for words. Writing things down was difficult, and reading didn't make any sense. She could see the squiggles, and she knew they were letters, but to her it appeared like a jumbled mess on the page. The other children found this funny and they'd call her names because of it. But to Emma it was a daily chore. She much preferred the joys of drawing, of filling the page with wild patterns and a bright rainbow of colour.

'If only I had my sketchbook. I wish I could draw this!' she said.

'You can!' yelled Tat. 'Draw it in here,' and she tapped the side of her head.

'In my head?'

Tat grinned. 'Yes silly. In your head. All you have to do is remember what you see for later. Now come with me!'

She pulled Emma up the nearest tree. Up, up they scrambled, beyond the squirrels and the chattering birds, up until it seemed that they would never stop. There was no end to it, just a ladder of trees, a tangle of branches poking in every direction.

'This is the highest I've ever been.' gasped Emma. She could see all four corners of the wood, and every animal in it.

'Now we shall fly!' Tat cried. She let out a wail and jumped, and the strangest thing happened. The tree to the left stuck out its branch to catch her.

'You try!' she called, but Emma was scared.

'I can't,' she said. 'What if I fall?'

'You won't,' Tat smiled. 'The trees are magic. They won't let you.'

Emma sighed. It was hard to have confidence when you always got things wrong. How did you learn to just let go? She saw Tat's pleading eyes, her hand beckoning. This wasn't going to be easy, but if she closed her eyes, maybe held her breath a little …

'Come on, go for it!'

Tat's voice filled her head, go for it, you can do it. She forced down a gulp of air, and with her lungs puffed out and with her eyelids tight shut she sprang from the tips of her toes. Sure enough, the tree bent and caught her by the ankle.

'This is fun!' she laughed.

'Told you!' giggled Tat, and they continued to swing from tree to tree, like tiny chimps.

Soon they grew tired and found themselves resting at the edge of a sparkling brook. The water peered at them with huge red eyes.

'Who is this?' said the rippling voice.

'This is Emma, she's come to visit us.'

'And what does Emma see in my waters?'

Emma leant over the edge. She hoped she didn't have to read, but to her surprise a picture had formed.

'I see all the kids at school, and they are talking to me. Wow!'

'Well of course they are,' said Tat. 'Now come on, there's still a lot to do and so little time.'

Next they found the Wishing Well and asked it for a tale.

'The Wishing Well loves to talk,' said Tat, 'so whenever you pass it, it's only polite to stop and ask for a tale.'

Emma nodded. This was like a fairy tale, and she was at the centre of it all.

'Make a wish, and make it good.' The Wishing Well's voice sent a tremble into the golden heart of the Forest.

'Well I wouldn't mind some food,' said Emma. 'Some ice-cream and chocolate cake.'

'And jelly, and gingerbread too,' giggled Tat.

'Oh yes please.'

No sooner had they made their wish than it appeared, on a strawberry-checked cloth at their feet.

'Wow! What a feast! I can't wait to tell everyone back home!'

'Home,' sighed Tat. 'Do you have to go?'

But they both knew the answer to that.

'You could come with me,' said Emma, 'I'd love to show you my world.'

Tat nodded. 'I'd like that too.'

'Of course, it isn't magic like yours.'

'Everywhere has some magic, I'm sure we can find some in your world.'

So when they were almost full to the brim, they wrapped up their plates in the cloth and dropped it into the well, with a 'thank you'. Then they walked around the oak tree again.

'Three times round, and three times old,
From the forest made of gold!'
they sang.

Again an opportunity for the class to join in and either repeat the phrase above or use their own.

And there they were again, popped into the playground like nothing had happened.

'I wonder why no one else sees me?' asked Tat.

'It must be because they're not really looking,' said Emma.

'So what now?'

'Now,' Emma smiled, 'we go to lessons!'

It was such a good feeling for Emma to finally have a friend with her instead of sitting by herself. To know that there was someone she could laugh with, instead of facing the jibes of her classmates. It didn't matter that they couldn't see Tat. She knew Tat was there and that gave her the confidence to sit, head high, face beaming.

'What's up with dumbo?' Jake Patterson sniggered. 'Don't know why you pretend to read, we all know you're stupid.'

'Who's he?' whispered Tat.

Emma's eyes glistened. She didn't want to cry in front of her new friend but Jake had a way of making her stomach churn.

'His name's Jake. He doesn't like me very much.'

'Well I don't like him!'

Tat crept mouse-like under the table until she reached Jake's feet. She worked deftly, her nimble fingers felt like feathers about his ankles. When she was done, she slipped from the floor and grasped Jake under his arms, her fingers tickling either side of his ribs. He let out a series of squeals, which sent the class into uproar.

'Jake Patterson!' the teacher shouted, 'If you've got something to say, stand up and say it.'

'I … I er, I'm sorry Miss.'

Tat tickled some more and this time he let out a loud yelp.

'Jake Patterson, come to the front of the class, now!'

He shoved back his chair and began to kick out a leg, but his shoelaces were tied in a knot. The class giggled as he teetered left then right before collapsing with a thud on his back.

'I wonder who looks stupid now!' said Tat as she slipped back beside her friend.

Emma grinned. She couldn't believe what fun she was having.

'Did you paint those pictures in your head like I told you to?' asked Tat.

'I think so. I've never tried to remember anything like that before. The First Forest is so beautiful.'

'Well, why don't you have a go at drawing it now?'

'I suppose I could.' Emma paused. 'I suppose art is a type of magic isn't it?'

'Oh yes,' said Tat. 'Come on, let's see what spells you can perform.'

For the next few minutes Emma worked on her picture. She traced with a pencil and then with some crayons. She worked on the curves and the lines, on the bark of the trees and the golden leaves that fell like confetti. She filled in the sky, and the soft mossy earth. She even drew the Wishing Well.

As she continued to weave with her pencil a crowd began to form, children leaning over their desks to get a look at her picture. Others gathered around, their mouths wide.

When I use this story I get the class to split into groups and draw the type of picture Emma might have created. I get them to think about the First Forest, and what it might look like. I ask them to write a few key words to help them describe the Forest and what they saw whilst they were there. It helps to follow this up with a discussion about the kind of wildlife, trees and plants you might find in a forest or woodland area.

'Emma, how did you do that?'

'That's so good.'

'I wish I could draw like that!'

She looked up, her eyes sparkling. 'You really like it?'

'Yes!' came back a chorus of replies.

'They like it, Tat. They like it!'

But when she looked to where her friend had been sitting there was only a space, an empty chair and the echo of laughter.

For days Emma looked for Tat. She drew wonderful pictures of her friend and the adventure they'd shared in the First Forest, but she never saw her again. Her pictures were so good that the other kids began to ask questions, and Emma found she could tell them tales through her sketches. She was no longer tied by words. She had the magic of pictures, and of her artistic talent to help her along. She made friends and felt accepted, even by the likes of Jake Patterson.

'I guess there is magic in this world,' she said one day, whilst putting the finishing touches to a painted image of Tat. And it was the strangest thing, because she thought she saw the red-haired girl on the page wrinkle her nose and wink back.

As a follow up activity, the class might want to create storyboards to describe their own adventures in the First Forest with Tat. Or perhaps they could think about what would happen if Tat visited their school. These could be written or verbal exercises.

The Water Lord – a traditional tale of good and evil

This is a story I made up for a session on witches in a primary school. I wanted it to be a moral tale, and I wanted the children to be able to identify with the lesson about greed. I also wanted to offer them the opportunity to join in at various points in the tale. I have highlighted these below.

There was once a great Water Lord, Emperor of all the rivers and the seas. He had the most amazing kingdom, filled with the rich colours of the seabed and the dancing lights of the fishes. He had many servants. You could say he had everything there was to have in his beautiful ocean world. But there was one thing that he longed for more than anything else. One thing that had always escaped him and that thing was love. The Water Lord yearned for a princess to take as his bride, to live with him beneath the sea for evermore. He had scoured the waters high and low, but he could not find what he was looking for.

Then one day he happened upon the sound of a maiden singing beside a river. She had the most beautiful voice he had ever heard, and so he rose up to the surface of the water just to get a glimpse of her. She was everything he could have imagined and more. She had hair like spun gold that fell about her waist. She had pale skin like moon flesh and eyes that shone like sapphires. The Water Lord was entranced. He tried to attract her attention, but all she saw were faint ripples at the water's edge. Each and every day the same thing happened. The Water Lord would hear her singing, he would rise to the edge of the river, but she failed to see him. As the days moved into weeks and the weeks moved into months he grew more and more frustrated. He had found his princess bride, but she didn't even know he was alive. In the end he did the only thing he could do. He ordered all the rivers and the seas to flood their banks, to claim the earth and everything upon it so that he could have his bride.

And so it was. The rivers and the seas rose high, higher than the tallest tree, and they broke their banks, and dragged away everything on land just as he had ordered. The Water Lord had his prize at last, but she was of little use to him for she lay on the ocean bed with her eyes closed and her skin pale.

Nothing he could do could rouse her from her sleep. He tried everything, he spoke to all his advisers, but no one could help him. Until eventually a small sea urchin spoke up.

'Your Greatness,' it said in a timid little voice, 'I believe there is someone who could help, someone who could make the girl smile and live and laugh again.'

'Who might that be?' asked the Water Lord in a booming voice. 'Who could bring her to life for me?'

'The Water Witch. She lives at the far side of the ocean in a cave but she is not to be trusted.'

'If that is the case,' said the Water Lord, 'then why will she choose to help me?'

'You must give her something in return. You must give her whatever she asks, and then she will cast a spell for you.'

The Water Lord smiled. 'Then so be it,' he said. 'Thank you my little friend.'

So the Water Lord carried the body of his princess through the sea, they swam on and on until eventually they reached the far side of the ocean. There the Water Lord saw the cave. It had a huge entrance, but instead of using this he chose to swim beneath the cave until he rose up through the centre of a small rock pool. He gently placed the body of the girl upon the rocks and waited. He could hear the sound of laughter in the distance; the sound of brittle bones moving. He could smell something sour like rotten fruit coming from the darkest depths of the cavern. Then he heard her. Her voice was harsh like razor blades and broken glass. When she came into view he held his breath. He had never seen anything quite so appalling. She had clumps of hair, and yellow eyes, and her teeth were chipped and brown. She had spots and pimples and a pointy chin, and she walked with a terrible limp.

'You there!' she pointed. 'What is it that you want of me?'

'I've come for your help. I need you to cast a spell so that my princess here can live with me beneath the sea.'

'And why should I do that?' she asked. 'What will you give me in return?'

'Whatever you want I will give you.'

The Witch smiled and it twisted her mouth into an ugly grimace. 'Let me think,' she said, and then 'I know, I know what I want ....'

'Give me more, give me more, I want gifts from the shore.

Give me jewels, make me rich, then I'll grant you your wish!'

The Water Lord frowned, 'But what riches can I bring you from the sea bed?'

'I don't know, but if you want me to cast you a spell, then you'll have to bring me something! Didn't you hear me? I said. ...'

You can get the class to join in with your chant at this point.

'Give me more, give me more, I want gifts from the shore.

Give me jewels, make me rich, then I'll grant you your wish!'

And with that she laughed and made her way back into the passages within her cave.

The Water Lord thought long and hard. What on earth could he bring her?

Ask the class to think about what gifts the Water Lord might bring from the sea. What might he find on the sea bed?

Then an idea came to him. Of course! Of course there were things he could bring the Witch. He blew his princess a chaste kiss and swam down through the rock pool and out into the ocean deep. He swam for what seemed like days, through stormy seas and billowing waves, until eventually he reached the ocean bed, and there he found an array of colourful stones, stones that shone and glistened like stars. He gathered them up in his arms and he swam back to the cave. When he got there, he placed the stones in the entrance and piled them up for the Witch to see. Then he waited.

Eventually the old crone appeared and she was even more hideous than before.

'So you've returned, and what have you brought for me?'

'I have collected the most beautiful stones from the ocean bed, look at them.' he said, and the Witch did look. She looked at the pile of stones that stood in the entrance to the cave.

'Very good,' she smiled, 'but not good enough!'

Then she took a deep breath and began to chant …

Again, get the class to join in with you and become the Witch.

'Give me more, give me more, I want gifts from the shore.

Give me jewels, make me rich, then I'll grant you your wish!'

The Water Lord sighed. What else could he get the witch?

Use this point to ask the children what other things the Water Lord might bring from the sea for the Witch.

Then he smiled. Yes, there was something else! With that he swam once more down through the rock pool and out into the ocean. Down into the very depths of the dark blue, and there he found what he was looking for; hundreds and thousands of pearls. Pearls from the sea bed, surely the Witch would appreciate this gift.

You might want to describe pearls and explain how they are found at this point.

He gathered all the pearls he could find and brought them back to the Witch's cave, and piled them high on the colourful stones in the entrance for the Witch to see.

'My, my,' the Witch said when she saw them. 'You have been busy, and how pretty everything looks!'

'Now you can cast me a spell and bring my princess to life.'

But the Witch shook her head. 'You think this is enough to satisfy me?' she laughed, and the sound echoed through the watery cave.

Again use this as an opportunity to get the children to join in with your chant.

'Give me more, give me more, I want gifts from the shore.

Give me jewels, make me rich, then I'll grant you your wish!'

'But what else can I bring you?' the Water Lord said sadly.

Then an idea came to him. Maybe there was one more thing.

Get the class to guess what the Water Lord might bring for the Witch this time.

So the Water Lord swam once more out of the cave going down through the rock pool. He swam on and on into the night, past the furthest point of the ocean, until he reached a golden beach. There he found what he was looking for.

What might that be? Ask the class.

There were thousands and millions of shells; shells of every shape and colour and size. The Witch would surely like these. He gathered as many as he could in his arms and swam back to the cave. Then he placed them on top of his other gifts. Now the entrance to the cave was so full, you could not see the sea or the daylight because the Witch had so many treasures.

'There, I have brought for you everything I can find in my kingdom. Now will you grant me my wish?'

The Witch smiled, 'I suppose so.'

She took out a silver wand and tapped it gently on the sleeping girl's legs. Then she said some strange words that made little sense to the Water Lord.

You could ask the class to make up the spell at this point.

Then the strangest thing happened. The dead girl's legs began to fuse together, until they looked like a golden fish tail, and her eyelids fluttered open and the colour returned to her cheeks.

'She's a mermaid!' the Water Lord gasped. 'Now she can live with me under the sea.'

And the mermaid looked at the Water Lord for the first time and she saw her prince, the one who had saved her, and she smiled.

That night, after leaving the Witch's cavern, the Water Lord and his bride were married. They had a huge feast beneath the sea and there was much merriment. In fact, in honour of this celebration the Water Lord once again ordered all the rivers and the seas to rise up and flood their banks. It was to be the best party of all. As the water began to rise, so did the water in the rock pool in the Witch's cave. It got higher and higher until it flooded the dark hole. Until the Witch was up to her ears with water! But there was no way out, for the entrance to her cave was still filled with all the gifts that the Water Lord had brought; all the gifts that had satisfied the Witch's greed.

Outside, a little sea urchin floated, and it listened to the last lingering splutters of the Witch crying for help. Then it swam away to join the festivities and to celebrate with the Water Lord and his new mermaid bride.

I finish this tale by asking what the moral was. There are several different lessons to be learnt.

Who was the most selfish, the Witch for her greed or the Water Lord for his own selfish desires?

To Be Me –
a Tat Rootwhistle tale

Shakeela tugged her long black hair behind her ears. She smoothed it with damp fingers before twisting it into a hair band. She hated tying it back, but that's what school expected. It was so unfashionable. She longed to try some of the funky styles, to cut her hair and colour it. That would be cool. Unfortunately her family had forbidden her from doing anything nearly as exciting.

'But it's my best feature!' she'd argue with her mother.

'It's not respectable. How can you want to cut it?'

'Because at least then I'll fit in.'

'And who wants to fit in? You should be proud of your culture.'

That's all she ever heard. You should be this; you should be that – what about what she wanted to be?

Her brothers laughed at her. They couldn't see her problem, but then things were different for them. They didn't have to be anything.

'What's up, Sis?' they'd cry in squeaky, babyish voices. That only made her ten times angrier.

At school things weren't easy. It wasn't that she didn't have friends. She had more than a few; in fact she was in one of the 'top' gangs, the crowds that ruled the roost. Her best friend Aisha said that was an honour, that being part of this gang meant you had to set the standard for the younger kids. Aisha was so trendy. She'd had her Afro hair straightened and highlighted. She wore fuchsia pink lip-gloss and designer trainers. Shakeela wished she could be more like Aisha. She had attitude.

'I just ask my dad for the money. He wouldn't say no to me.'

'My dad would,' frowned Shakeela. 'He doesn't let me do anything.'

'He's no right to stop you! You are your own person.'

'I wish.'

And so it went on, until one day Shakeela snapped. She'd felt it coming, felt the blood flushing her cheeks and the heat burning her neck. It was too hard to hold all that anger in any more. She'd spent the afternoon skiving off school with Aisha. They'd done the usual, dodging anyone who looked remotely like a teacher. They'd had fish and chips courtesy of Aisha's dad, and sat reading the latest issue of a gossip magazine on a park bench. Then it was time for the Shopping Centre. The usual thing happened. Aisha chose a target; this time it was Lucy's, an accessories shop on the main stretch. Lucy's was like a treasure trove. Shakeela gasped at all the bangles and baubles and hair bands.

'Wow, I love those hair ties!' she said pointing to some pink taffeta bows.

'Take em' then' whispered Aisha.

'Oh I couldn't.'

'Yes you could. It's easy. You've seen me do it before now.'

'I know, but I just don't think I could. What if I get caught?'

Aisha grinned, 'With me by your side, it just isn't going to happen girl.'

Shakeela took a breath. Maybe this was her chance? She wanted to fit in with the rest of the gang, and really she could never afford anything as nice as this. If she did okay then next time she could try her hand at some designer trainers, just like Aisha's.

'I'll do the usual,' nodded Aisha. 'Just follow my lead.'

Shakeela smiled. 'Okay, I'm with you.'

The shop assistant looked like she was sucking a lemon. Her eyes were hard, her mouth turned down at the edges. Shakeela ignored her and made her way to the stand with the hair ties. They really were pretty. Aisha was just in front of her, near a box full of rings. The sound came first, the clattering noise as Aisha grabbed a handful and sent the box flying. Shakeela screamed. The noise flipped her stomach and she yanked the hair tie from its plastic container. They both ran, barging into two other shoppers. Shakeela could feel her heart drumming, the sound made her head throb. She continued to run, sailing through the Centre and out onto the street, around the corner and across the road. She glanced behind her, but there was no sign of Aisha. Had she been caught? Had she gone a different way? Shakeela began to panic. She turned back just in time to see herself crashing head first into a tree. The rough bark grazed her face and sent her spinning forwards, but the final thump never came. Instead she found that she was still running inside the tree! How could this be? Everything had a soft glow. It was like a meadow, the warm grass pricked at her ankles and the sun danced above her eyes. She could see valleys and hills dotted with

buttercups, and in the distance trees, like silver arrows pointing to the sky.

'Oh no!' Shakeela gasped. 'Where   am I?'

'In a tree!' came the reply. The voice was female, and of about the same age, but it had a funny singsong ring to it. Shakeela stopped for a moment and rubbed her eyes. When she opened them she could see a girl with a cloud of red untidy hair standing before her. Her face was peppered with freckles, her eyes shaped like almonds and sparkling green.

'You took quite a knock coming through there!' the girl added.

'I did? Who are you?'

'The name's Tat, Tat Rootwhistle. Who are you?'

'Shakeela Lal.'

Tat leaned forward and scooped up the pink hair tie from the earth with her fingers. 'What's this?'

'Hey, that's mine!' Shakeela snapped. 'I must have dropped it.'

'Really? Oh I'm sorry. I've never seen anything like this before. What's it for?'

Shakeela slumped down. Her head hurt and she felt a bit giddy.

'It's for your hair.'

'I see.'

'You haven't seen my friend have you? She was supposed to be following me.'

'No, I didn't see anyone come through here but you, and you were in quite a hurry!'

'I had to get away,' Shakeela said, remembering what she had done. It didn't feel good at all.

'Why? Is somebody after you?'

'I've done a bad thing. I wish I hadn't done it, but I thought it might make me like them.'

'Like who?' Tat wrinkled her nose.

'Part of the gang. Oh I've made such a mess of everything. I just wanted to be accepted.'

Tat nodded.

'You see my dad won't let me wear trainers or make-up or colour my hair like the other girls. He says it's wrong. But I want to; I'm fed up of him telling me what to do. Aisha said if I did this, then I'd be really cool like her.'

Tat smiled. 'And why would you want to be like everyone else? It's more fun just being you.'

'I suppose.' Shakeela sighed. 'But now what am I going to do?'

'You're going to come with me!' grinned Tat.

'But I need to get home.'

'And you will,' said Tat. 'In the meantime I've got something to   show you.'

It was strange being inside a tree, but stranger still when she felt her body raise from the ground. It was like being lifted on invisible wings and carried through the air. She closed her eyes, not daring to look down. She could feel Tat's hand in hers, could sense her legs being stretched.

'This is weird. Am I flying?' she whispered.

'In a way!' Tat sang.

She could feel her ponytail flowing behind her. The touch of wind cooling her cheeks, and then quite suddenly everything stopped. Her feet touched the ground in a gliding motion and Tat nipped her arm.

'Where are we?' asked Shakeela.

'You'll know soon enough.'

They were standing outside a house, not unlike Shakeela's home. It was part of an estate; its red-bricked front had the same green door and small slab of garden. The only difference was where her front lawn was neatly mowed with flowerbeds this garden was a sprawling mass of weeds. The door was ajar and Tat slipped inside, her arm looped through Shakeela's.

'Don't worry, they can't see or hear you,' she said.

Shakeela watched open-mouthed. In the living room a large man lay on the sofa. A younger boy was on the phone.

'That's Aisha's brother, I'm sure of it!'

Tat nodded. They watched as the boy put down the phone.

'Dad, Aisha's in trouble. She's been caught stealing again.'

'So?' the man sighed. 'What am I supposed to do about it?'

'They want you to go down the police station and get her.'

'They can think again. I'm busy.'

He flicked through the TV channels, settling on some wrestling.

'But Dad, we can't just leave her there.'

'Look, I let you do what you want, so you let me do what I want, okay? Now get out of here!'

The boy muttered something under his breath, then left the room.

Outside Shakeela shook her head. She couldn't believe that this was how Aisha lived.

'Doesn't he care about her?' she asked.

'It seems not.'

'I don't understand. She said her dad gave her money for everything!'

'Perhaps he does,' said Tat. 'It doesn't mean that he cares.'

'No, I suppose it doesn't.'

Shakeela felt sad. All this time she'd imagined what it would be like to be Aisha, to be accepted as part of the gang and have anything she wanted. But it didn't matter. How could it? Without the love of her parents, without knowing that they cared, nothing else counted.

'It's not about the labels is it? Or the make-up or clothes?'

Tat shrugged. 'I don't know. I wish I could say, but this isn't my world'

'So what's it like in your world?'

Tat's face lit up. 'The First Forest, that's where I come from. It's a wonderful place. You can go tree jumping for hours and still find new places to explore! You can talk to the animals and make magical wishes. You can do anything you want, if you've a mind to.'

'Sounds like fun.'

'It is,' said Tat. 'Maybe I'll take you one day. But for now we must go back. There are people looking for you.'

Shakeela scratched her head. 'How do you know that?'

'I just do!'

Once again Tat had her by the hand, lifting her high up into the summer breeze.

Shakeela closed her eyes, and enjoyed feeling weightless like a feather. She thought this was something pretty special; something even better than being in a gang. When they landed it was with a harsh crack. Shakeela opened her eyes, to find herself in totally different surroundings. She was in bed, in hospital, or at least it looked like a hospital from what she remembered of having her tonsils out. She felt a hand squeeze her own lightly.

'Tat?' she asked. Her vision was blurred but the face slowly came into view.

'Shakeela darling, we've been so worried.'

It was her mum, and then at the foot of the bed her dad leaned forward.

'You really gave us a scare you know. We're so glad you're all right.'

'How did I end up here? I was at Aisha's house.'

Her parents frowned at each other. 'Aisha's in a lot of trouble, but we won't talk about that now,' her father said.

'We're just so happy to have you back,' her mother said. 'You took quite a bang on your head according to the doctors.'

'I did?'

'Yes, I don't know how it happened, but at least you're okay.'

'I'm sorry,' she said. Her eyes were watering.

'Oh, Shakeela, you do know we only want the best for you?'

'I know dad, and really, all that stuff I said was wrong. I don't want to cut my hair, I don't want to change anything about myself.'

Her father nodded. 'You're perfect as you are. You've a lot to be proud about; don't worry about what other people think.'

'I won't, not ever again.'

She smiled. Tat had taught her that. If only she'd had the chance to   thank her.

'Dad?'

'Yes, Shakeela.'

'When I get out of here, can I have Aisha around for tea? I know she's done some bad things, but I think she needs a friend right now.'

Her father smiled. 'Yes, I think you could be right.'

Tat listened to the whispers on the wind, the sounds of the trees in deep conversation, and the soft rhythmic dance of earth beneath her feet. She loved the First Forest. It was hard to pull away sometimes. She scrambled to the edge of the stream and let her toes dangle in the silvery waters. The reflection that smiled back had the same cheeriness and a wild glint of 'adventure' in her eyes. There in the centre of her candyfloss hair, a pink hair tie fluttered. She wasn't sure what it was for, but it looked sweet and it reminded her of the girl she'd met in her dreams, earlier that day.

The Friendship Game – a Tat Rootwhistle tale

The computer blinked, the screen popped and a flame stretched across to signal it was ready for action. Joshua settled into gaming mode, his face almost pressed against the pictures. He loved his computer more than anything else. It was the one time he felt safe, and in control. It didn't matter what game he was playing, he knew them all so well, and that was a good feeling. He didn't have to guess. He could just sit and pretend. He wished life was more like a game, because then he'd be in charge, he'd have no one telling him what to do. There'd be no need for school, or homework, because it would all be about getting to the next level.

Of course, he couldn't expect his parents to understand. They thought it was silly and a waste of time. They had bought him the computer and games module for his birthday a year ago. He'd begged them over and over, and as he'd reasoned, all his friends had one. Surely they wouldn't want him to be the odd one out? He had promised that it wouldn't interfere with his schoolwork, and at first it didn't. But that's because he hadn't known what fun it was, how exciting to lose yourself so completely in something. He didn't have to imagine because the images were there, parading their tales of terror and intrigue right before his eyes. It became a ritual, something he had to do every night after tea. And then it progressed to the mornings before school. He started getting up earlier just so that he could play a game, move on to the next stage. It gave him something to talk about with his friends, but after a while even they didn't understand. You see nothing was sacred. Sleep was for babies; he didn't need all that time in bed. Instead he would sneak out from under the covers, and play his games by torchlight. He'd never realised how handy the flashlight his dad had bought him would become!

Soon his parents became concerned.

'It's not normal,' he overheard his mum telling his dad.

'It's affecting his studies.'

'But it's only a bit of fun, I mean, all kids play these computer games, don't they?'

'Maybe so, but not as much as Josh does. He's becoming obsessed. I'm really worried.'

'I'll have a word with him,' his dad had said.

And Joshua had smiled; he would be ready for him.

'It's only a bit of fun, Dad,' he'd said. 'I always make sure I do my work first. I've been doing it in the break times, honestly.'

'Well just as long as you do, lad. You know how your mother worries.'

And that had been the end of it for a while. But how could Joshua explain to them? The games had become his life. If he left them now, there'd be nothing but a well, a vast space inside with nothing to fill it.

It was very early as he watched his computer go through the usual set up procedure. The birds had been tweeting their morning song, but it was still dark, and with the curtains closed the bedroom looked almost eerie. The light from the computer cast a green glow on his desk, and from the book shelf the small flashlight provided a white dot of brightness. Joshua began to set up his favourite game; the one where the hero had to follow the clues to find the treasure. He was already on the last stage and each time his performance improved.

'Nobody understands,' he muttered, 'I couldn't give you up. I just couldn't.'

His fingers tapped quickly, he licked dry lips and outside the bird song increased.

The game was loading. A few more minutes and he would be back in the forest, where he'd left his character. Buzz and bleep, the computer struggled, the light dimmed and flashed.

'Come on!' Joshua urged.

But the computer seemed to be fighting, having an argument with itself. The buzzing noise continued, building up until it filled his head. He rubbed his eyes. He was tired, but he had to finish this level.

'Come on, stupid computer!'

The buzzing was almost as loud as the birds. In fact the cheeping of the birds was all around him now. It felt like they were pecking at his brain, their sharp beaks interrupting his concentration. Joshua squeezed his eyes shut.

'Stop it!' he cried.

'Stop what?' came the voice in his ear.

He turned around to find the strangest girl he'd ever seen sitting on his bed. She had berry red hair like a giant bird's nest, and a pointed chin that was cocked to one side.

'Am I dreaming?' he asked.

'I don't think so, but let's check.' And with that the girl leaned over and pinched him hard on his right arm.

'Ouch!'

'See, you're not dreaming,' she grinned. 'I could have told you that.'

She watched him, her leaf green eyes wide with excitement. 'Isn't this fun? I don't know quite how I got here, but I like an adventure.'

'Well you can't stay,' Joshua grumbled.

'Whyever not?'

'Because I'm busy.' Joshua motioned to his computer, the screen still a solid square of darkness.

'Oh that. Well I don't think it's working. I think that's how I ended up here, I came through that. One minute I was in the First Forest and the next I'm here. Anyway, what's your name? Mine's Tat, Tat Rootwhistle.'

'That's a silly name,' said Joshua, his face flushed with confusion and anger at the interruption.

'Well what's yours?'

'Joshua.'

Tat rose from the bed and walked over to the computer screen. 'What is this anyway, a box?'

'Ssh!' Joshua said. 'You'll wake my parents.'

'Oh sorry. I forget sometimes. Where I come from it doesn't matter how loud you shout.'

'And where do you come from?' Joshua asked. He knew this was all far-fetched and that there had to be some explanation for the wild girl in his room, but now he was interested.

'I come from a place beyond time, Joshua. A place of giant talking trees, and grasses that stretch beneath your feet. And the animals that live there are my friends. They talk to me, tell me their tales.'

'Animals can't talk!'

'Oh you're so wrong. Everything can talk, it's just that we've forgotten how to listen.'

Joshua frowned.

'I think you should go now. I need to sort out what's wrong with my computer.'

'Is that was this is?' And she prodded the empty screen. 'Doesn't seem to be doing much.'

'That's because you've broken it, when you came through.'

'Oh dear,' Tat sighed. 'Well I didn't mean to do that. Is there any way I can help?'

'You can go back to wherever it is you live, and leave me alone.'

Tat scratched her rachetty head, causing bits of moss to fall on the carpet.

'You're not very friendly are you? Still, if all you do all day is stare at that thing, I'm not surprised.'

'Look, I didn't ask for you to turn up here like you did. This is my bedroom!'

'Alright, alright.' She tried to force a smile, but he could tell she was upset. 'I can tell you don't want company. I'll go.'

And with that she spun around three times and disappeared, leaving Josh with his mouth open.

The rest of the day was a blur to Josh. He was upset that his computer wasn't working, and he was confused about his early morning visitor. Had he made it up? Was he seeing things? She'd seemed real enough, with her wild bushy hair and brittle stick-like limbs. He'd felt the heat from her touch, and the smell of freshly cut grass had filled his room long after she'd gone. He couldn't wait to get home and turn his computer on; perhaps she'd pop through again? Hopefully his computer would be fixed and he'd be able to play to his heart's content. But when he got home nothing had changed.

'Never mind,' Josh's mother had said later that night when he told her his computer wasn't working. 'We'll get it fixed, but in the meantime you could always read a book.'

Read a book, read a stuffy book, Joshua thought. How could she say that?

He just didn't know what to do. He felt empty and alone. He lay on his bed, legs curled beneath him and his head pressed against the soft pillows. Slowly his eyes drifted shut, the shadows of the night sky casting patterns against his eyelids. He wanted to cry. His stomach was in knots, and his fingers felt useless. The smell of the garden filled his throat, and he shivered from the cool breeze that whipped at his legs. Had he left the window open? He was about to climb off the bed to see when he realised that he wasn't lying in bed at all. Instead a lumpy mound of grass cushioned him. And when he looked up all he could see were tall willowy trees reaching far beyond the sky. The shock made him cry out, and that was when the muddy earth rumbled.

'Who is it that dares to disturb *my* sleep?'

Josh jumped up, his skin prickled by fear.

'Who's there?'

'I'm asking the questions little boy,' the voice boomed.

'But I can't see you!' Josh squeaked.

'That doesn't mean I don't exist. Don't they teach you anything at school?'

Joshua shrugged; he'd not really paid much attention to what they told him in his lessons. He'd always been too busy thinking about the next game.

'I'm sorry,' Josh said, studying his toes.

'Good. If you want to know who I am just take a look around you. I'm everything you see. I'm the spirit of the First Forest. Now you can tell me who you are, and why you've come into my kingdom.'

Joshua held his breath. How could he answer? He didn't have a clue how he'd ended up there.

'My name's Josh.'

'Speak up, boy!' the forest spirit ordered.

'I said, I'm called Josh, and I don't know how I ended up here. I was in bed because my computer wouldn't work and the next thing I know I'm here.'

The ground shook and shuddered and Joshua realised that the spirit had found his explanation amusing.

'It's not funny!'

'Oh I think it is.' The spirit went on, 'I've heard all about you. You're the computer boy aren't you? The one who can't be bothered to make friends any more.'

'Who told you?'

'Who do you think?' the ground said. 'Don't you remember anything except your games? Oh you really are in a bad way.'

'I don't have to listen to this,' Josh said walking between the trees.

'It doesn't matter where you go, I'm everywhere. I am this forest. The only way to get away from me is to leave, and you can't do that.'

'But I want to go home!' Josh slumped next to a tall quivering oak and began to cry.

'Then you have to treat this like one of your games,' the Spirit answered.

'And how do I do that?'

But the spirit had gone, leaving the wind to answer with a gust of leaves.

Joshua sat in silence. Treat this like a game, he thought. But how could it be a game, he was stuck somewhere he didn't want to be? In fact he didn't even know where he was. It was hard to see anything with the clambering trees and the dense undergrowth. He needed a better view. Perhaps the forest was only a small part of where he was, and there were people living beyond this place who could help him. In a game if he needed help he'd take a step back and see the picture from the outside.

He looked up into the gnarled branches of the nearest tree. It had lots of dents and cracks, plenty of footholds, should someone care to climb it. He began rolling up his jeans, and then he made a grab for the first branch. It was firm and strong and he let out a sigh of relief. He'd never climbed a tree before. Steadily he wove in between the branches, his feet rubbing against the swarthy bark. It smelt good. The further he climbed the sweeter the juice from the tree. Insects circled him, wonderfully patterned butterflies and birds. It felt like they were encouraging him to climb higher. His breath was shallow but instead he thought about the beautiful view that would greet him at the top. He looked at the birds and laughed as they pecked and chirped playfully. This really wasn't that bad after all. His hands were dirty and rough but he liked the feeling. He stretched this way and that. The bending boughs moved with the breeze and there was a faint whiff of honey to the air. And soon he realised that he couldn't see the top of the tree. Where did it end? He paused for a better look at the surrounding land. There were trees, thousands of them, like a great hall of old wizards gathered in conference. Their rugged necks wavered, and their wrinkled hats reached in every direction.

'I'll never reach the top,' he muttered.

And then to the left of his eye, he caught a flicker of movement. A red darting light, a crackle of leaves, and soon he could see it was Tat flying through the trees at top speed.

'Tat, Tat!' he called, but she didn't hear him.

And again, 'Tat, Tat!' but still she dived and spun through the web of branches like a flame-feathered bird. This was the place she had talked about, the place she came from. She will know, she'll know where I am and what I should do, he thought. And at that point he wished he hadn't been so rude to her. He had to catch her attention. He had to say sorry. There was only one thing for it. If he jumped and made it to the next tree he'd be near enough to attract her attention. But if he missed, well it didn't bear thinking about. If he missed he'd fall into the murky depths of the forest, and it was quite a drop. He remembered then how in the games he'd been able to make the characters do anything he wanted. But it was always so easy, just the flick of a switch, or the tap of a key. But this, this was all down to him. If he didn't make the jump then he wouldn't be able to stop the game and start again. His chance would be over.

Gritting his teeth, Josh took a breath. He could feel his legs trembling. I can do this, he thought, I can do this. He swung back his arms, bent his legs and with a roaring cry of 'Taaaaat!!!' He let himself soar through the air.

The next thing that happened surprised him. He could feel small hands about his waist, and things gripping his clothes. His T-shirt was yanked and his jeans were lifted. Something soft brushed the skin of his arm. And then he felt the flapping sensation, air being pumped all around him. He was flying. He let his eyes fall open.

'Oh no,' he said, for there at all four corners were birds tugging at him through his clothes, and Tat beneath pushing him upwards.

'What's happening?'

But before he could be answered the next tree came into view, and a croaky voice gushed, 'Thank Heavens for that.'

He could feel himself land on a small plateau of twigs and moss, still high up in the branches, but resting.

'Joshua, whatever made you do that?' It was Tat's voice in his ear.

'I, I, wanted to say hello.'

'There are other ways you know. You could have just shouted, Hello Tat.'

'I did, you didn't hear me!'

She shrugged, 'Well at least you're in one piece anyway, what are you doing here? I thought you didn't want to be friends.'

Josh flushed in shame. 'I'm sorry. I was a bit rude wasn't I? I didn't mean to be. I was upset about my computer. But I don't really know how I've ended up here. I was sulking, I suppose, because my computer didn't work. One minute I was on my bed with my eyes closed, the next minute I was here.'

'Oh, that's not so good. Folks don't usually come here unless there's a reason.'

Josh scratched his head. 'Where are we anyway?'

'In the First Forest, silly. I told you about it. It's my home and the kind of place anything can happen.'

'Oh I know.' And Josh began telling the story of the earth spirit and how he'd climbed the tree to find out where he was. 'I thought maybe you could help me find my way back,' he said finally. 'I feel a fool for being so nasty before.'

Tat grinned and he noticed how her features shone like the moon and how her hair seemed to be alive with tiny woodland creatures.

'That's okay. We all make mistakes. I can show you your way back. I can take you as easy as saying one, two, three.'

'That's great,' Josh smiled, 'but first I'd like to explore some more. I'd like you to show me some of these talking animals.'

'You would? Oh I can show you that and so much more.'

And with that she grabbed Josh's hand and plunged down into the heart of the forest.

Time passed quickly in the First Forest, and Josh knew that he had to get back before his parents missed him. He'd had such fun. Tat had taken him to meet all sorts of creatures, from the graceful racing deer with the soft singing voice, to the quirky mischievous squirrels, who spoke in short broken words and enjoyed playing vanishing tricks.

'It's been fun,' he said, 'but I have to go.'

'I know,' smiled Tat. 'And perhaps when you get back your computer will be fixed, yes?'

'My computer. I'd forgotten all about that.' Josh stopped then, and took one final look around him. 'There's one thing that's bugging me. I still don't know how I got here.'

'That's easy,' came the rumbling voice he'd heard before. 'I brought you here.'

Tat giggled, 'That's the Earth Spirit all right. Always sticking his nose in where it's not wanted.'

'That's not true Tat, I thought the boy deserved to know what it was like on the other side. He needed a friend, and I know no better than you.'

This time they all laughed.

Things were different on Josh's return. He'd enjoyed himself more than he'd ever imagined. It was great to get outside and go a little bit wild, to feel the wind against his cheeks and the dirt upon his hands. His computer was still there, and in a few days his parents had it fixed. But it didn't thrill him so much. The games were all the same. They didn't challenge him. He decided that there were other exciting things to discover, things that could be found in the park and the playground. His parents were delighted with the changes in Josh. They thanked their lucky stars that his computer had broken, because that had been the start of this new wave of outside interests. Of course, Josh knew different. He knew about the magical First Forest, and a wild girl with tatty red hair who roamed its pathways. He also knew that the earth talked, and that it made sense to listen.

The Music Man – a traditional ghost story

This story is adapted from a tale I found in a book set in Jamaica, a folk tale I believe. I decided to re-write it in a format that was suitable for a modern younger audience. I have tried to make it relevant to today. This is something that you can do with any story, if you think it has the potential for a storytelling session adapt it to suit your needs. It's essentially a ghost tale, and ideal for performing around Halloween.

Scott was a rock star. At least that's what he thought. Ever since his father bought him his first guitar for his ninth birthday he'd been hooked. It was like it was a part of him, like he had another arm, an arm that was bright red and electric and wailed powerful riffs on demand. He played it constantly, at home, at school, at break time. At first the class had thought it odd, but given time even they could see that Scott had a talent. He could play any song; it was as if he had magic fingers that could search out the right notes. After a time Scott set up his own band with two brothers, Ed and John. They practised every Thursday night at the brothers' house (Scott's mum enjoyed the peace for one night). And some nights the music clattered and crashed and didn't go quite as well, and other nights it gelled. It was as if everything fell into place and they cooked up a storm in the back bedroom with chaotic riffs and hypnotic tunes that seemed to go on forever.

It was one such night when the music flowed and time seemed to run away with itself when Scott looked at his watch and realised it was way past his bedtime.

'Sorry, lads. Time to go.'

He hadn't realised how fast the night had gone, but the melodies had been rich and sweet, the best they'd ever done. So Scott began his journey home with a smile on his face. Scott's house was only two streets away, so it wasn't far to go, and he didn't want to trouble his mum for a lift. Instead he swung his guitar on his shoulder and started to walk. But the strange thing was that in the hours that had passed the fog had come down and it was thicker than Scott had ever seen.

He could barely make out his hand in front of his face. Everything looked strange. The streets were all wrong. Shapes loomed ahead; thick claggy hands seem to grip at him, spectral fingers nipping his skin. The air was thick and he felt like he was walking in soup, thick damp soup.

He stopped for a moment and tried to make out the street ahead, but he didn't recognise it. Instead it seemed that he was standing in a vast wood, a wood with trees that shook and trembled. Shadows flickered in the distance. Scott took a breath. This was not good. He was lost and he could feel fear snaking up his spine. There was only one thing for it. He needed to calm himself, he needed to think logically and the only way he could do that was to play his guitar.

He lifted the strap over his head and positioned his fingers on the strings. He closed his eyes and began to play and the music that escaped was more wild and free than anything he had played before. It carried over his head, high into the trees. It lifted and dropped, it crashed like waves on a beach. It echoed everywhere in this strange foggy landscape. When Scott had finished he noticed that the mist had cleared a little. He could make out the shadowy shape of a man stood to the right of him. The man was tall and lean with a big floppy hat.

'Hey son, that was good. You play a mean guitar,' the Stranger said.

'Thanks,' said Scott. 'I love my guitar.'

'I can see that,' said the Stranger. 'So what are you doing out on such a terrible night?'

Now Scott was a sensible boy and he knew not to talk to strangers, but there was something different about this man. He felt like he knew him from somewhere.

'I'm lost,' admitted Scott, 'I started walking home and the fog got thicker and now, well now I'm really lost.'

'I see,' said the Stranger. 'Well maybe I can help you. If you let me play that there guitar, just for a minute or two, then perhaps I can put you on the right path.'

Scott wouldn't normally let anyone touch his guitar, but this Stranger was almost magical and Scott knew that he had a good heart. He didn't know how he knew, maybe it was something to do with the music, but he knew that everything would be all right. So taking a deep breath he lifted the guitar from his shoulders and passed it over. The Stranger nodded, took the guitar in his hands and began to play.

Scott had never heard music like it. It was beautiful; it started off like a lullaby then swept through the air like a violent breeze. It was hard and fast and enchanting. The notes seemed to press down on his eyes and before long his eyelids closed. He felt like he was being buffeted on the wind, like he was twisting and turning like a leaf. He saw animals running, he saw dragons breathing fire, he saw flames and water and dancing trees. He felt like he was dancing, spinning around and around, over and over and his heart was beating so fast. It was like a drum in time with the music. Then suddenly, just as suddenly as the first notes had begun, it stopped, and there was silence. Scott opened his eyes.

'Wow,' he said. 'How did that happen?'

Scott was standing before his front door. He was home at last!

The Stranger tipped his hat. 'Must have been the magic of the music.' he said. Then he passed the guitar back to Scott.

'But I don't understand. How can music be magic?'

'Well of course it's magic Scott. Music can do all sorts of things. It can lift people; it can make them feel happy or sad. It can call to people and things.'

Scott shrugged, and then a thought hit him.

'How did you know my name?'

'I know lots of things,' the Stranger said.

'Well you certainly can play the guitar. It was awesome.'

The Stranger laughed, 'You think so? Well you should have seen me when I was alive, then I could *really* play.'

With that he turned three times as if dancing on the wind and disappeared, leaving only a spiral of smoke in the air.

Bibliography and Further Resources

Davies, A.L.R. (2005) Story as a Tool for Learning. *Mathematics Teaching* 191 (June). Available at www.atm.org.uk/mt/archive/mt191/html.

Davies, A.L.R. (2005) Storytelling in Primary Schools. *Teaching and Learning Magazine* (June). Birmingham: Questions Publishing.

Pellowksi, A. (1991) *The World of Storytelling*, revised and expanded edition. Bronx, NY: H.W. Wilson.

Seely Brown, J., Denning, S,. Groh, K. and Prusak, L. (2004) *Storytelling in Organizations: How Narrative and Storytelling Are Transforming 21st Century Management*. Oxford: Butterworth Heinemann.

Further Resources

www.sfs.org.uk/
The Society for Storytelling web pages.

www.storyarts.org/
A fantastic web resource with articles and ideas for storytelling in the classroom.

www.creativekeys.net/StorytellingPower/sphome.html
A brilliant website with recommendations for reading material and ideas on how to incorporate stories into your life.

www.alisonlrdavies.com
Author's website, with articles on storytelling, fiction and contact details.